The Macat Library
世界思想宝库钥匙丛书

解析米尔顿·弗里德曼
《货币政策的作用》

AN ANALYSIS OF
MILTON FRIEDMAN'S
THE ROLE OF MONETARY POLICY

Nick Broten ◎ 著

陈虎 ◎ 译

上海外语教育出版社
外教社 SHANGHAI FOREIGN LANGUAGE EDUCATION PRESS

目　录

CONTENTS

引言

要点

- 米尔顿·弗里德曼是美国经济学家，诺贝尔经济学奖＊获得者，20世纪最具影响力的经济思想家之一。他的主要贡献涉及消费理论（销售与购买分析）、货币经济学＊（研究政府控制经济体中货币供应量时所产生的影响），以及经济学方法论（研究经济学所用的各种方法）。

- 弗里德曼的论文《货币政策的作用》概括了20世纪五六十年代通行货币政策＊所存在的各类问题，强调了政府利用货币供应＊与利率＊调节经济增长＊与失业＊时所面临的各种危险。

- 该文是20世纪经济决策领域的最为重要的论述之一，是货币主义＊学派的奠基之作。该学派主张，调节经济体中的流通货币总量可产生诸多优势。

米尔顿·弗里德曼其人

《货币政策的作用》一文的作者米尔顿·弗里德曼（1912—2006）是人类历史上最具影响力的经济学家之一。在他漫长而成果丰硕的学术生涯中，其重要学术贡献所涉及的领域包括宏观经济学＊（研究如何界定经济以及经济在宏观层面如何运行）、消费理论＊（大体而言，是指研究销售与购买的理论）、经济学方法论（即研究经济学所用的各种方法），以及经济史。

除了学术研究之外，弗里德曼也以积极支持自由市场＊经济学和个人自由而著称。他的公共演讲和著述，尤其是《资本主义与自由》（1962）及《自由选择》（1980）等著作，向公众传播了其意志自由论＊主张（指个人应享有充分自由并尽量减少政府干涉），并推动了自由市场思想的普及。

1912 年，弗里德曼出生于美国纽约市的一个第一代东欧犹太*移民家庭。尽管家境并不富裕，但父母教导弗里德曼要志向远大、自强自立。1932 年，弗里德曼从新泽西州的罗格斯大学毕业，正值史称"大萧条"*的灾难性经济崩溃。无论从经济层面，还是知识层面，这次衰退的种种影响都为弗里德曼的整个职业生涯提供了宝贵经验。对于这段时期，弗里德曼曾说："尽管我在芝加哥大学的第一年——1932 年至 1933 年，是我在经济上最为拮据的一年，但是就知识而言，这一年却为我开启了通往新世界的大门……"。[1]

继 1933 年获得芝加哥大学经济学硕士学位之后，1946 年弗里德曼又获得哥伦比亚大学经济学博士学位，同年开始在芝加哥大学担任全职教师。

与芝加哥大学的关系是弗里德曼学术声誉的重要组成部分。弗里德曼是"芝加哥经济学派"*的核心成员。该学派成员均为与芝加哥大学有关联的学者，他们主张政府不应干预经济，并对价格理论*兴趣浓厚。价格理论认为，一件物品的价值取决于供（获得该物品的难易程度）求（该物品的市场需求）关系。

芝加哥学派还主张对宏观经济政策（即针对整个经济体的经济政策）采取货币主义的方式。在《货币政策的作用》一文中，弗里德曼列举了上述政策的诸多内容。

与芝加哥学派的关系，对于弗里德曼的学术声誉既有助益，亦有损害。一方面，作为学派的领军人物之一，弗里德曼的学术观点得以影响更广泛的受众，很可能超越了他个人学术著作本身的影响。但另一方面，学派及其主要倡导者一直饱受来自左翼*的批评。例如，加拿大作家与社会活动家娜奥米·克莱因*就对芝加哥学派所主张的自由市场思想发出了反对的声音。[2]

《货币政策的作用》的主要内容

《货币政策的作用》一文于 1968 年发表，该文对此前的货币政策（即政府对于经济体中的货币供应量做出增加或限制的决定）观念提出了挑战。此前，人们认为，货币政策是实现通货膨胀 * 和失业率长期目标的有效工具。持此观点的是所谓的凯恩斯主义 * 经济学家，他们均认同英国经济学家约翰·梅纳德·凯恩斯 *（1883—1946）的主张，即政府对于公共事业的支出整体上对经济有利，因为可以刺激就业、提振需求，并促进经济增长。上述观点代表了弗里德曼的著作问世时最广为接受的经济学观念。

弗里德曼的批判目标十分明确：菲利普斯曲线 *。该理论由新西兰经济学家威廉·菲利普斯 * 提出，认为通货膨胀率与失业之间存在负相关。换言之，该理论认为，通货膨胀率升高，则失业降低，反之亦然。

1960 年，菲利普斯曲线由美国经济学家保罗·萨缪尔森 * 和罗伯特·索洛 * 合作完成推导。依据该曲线，货币政策可成为达成所需经济成果的工具。例如，如果货币当局（通常是一国的中央银行）想要降低失业，即可通过增加货币供应来达成目标。这是因为商品数量不变而货币增加，会推高通货膨胀。所以，通货膨胀与失业二者此消彼长、相互制约。

对于上述货币政策观点，弗里德曼并不完全认同，而是认为其太过乐观。他认为，上述观点忽略了一点，即当人们预期物价或工资水平发生变化时，其行为也会随之发生变化。同时，该观点还忽略了实际价值 * 与名义价值 * 之间的关键性差异。名义价值只是商品或服务的标称价值，而实际价值则需考虑随时间而发生的价格变化。例如，假定你的名义工资是每小时 10 美元，如果随后每年该工资水平保持不变但生活成本却不断上涨，那么，你的实际工资将会随时间而下降。弗里德曼将这一思想引入其对菲利普斯曲线的分析。

假定货币当局想要减少失业，根据菲利普斯曲线，提高通货膨胀率即可达成目标。由于商品价格的上涨速度一般会快于名义工资（即工人工资单上的实际数额）的增速，故会导致实际工资减少。但是，用不了多久，这一状况就会导致员工要求加薪或就此失业。这样，失业率就会重新升至之前的水平。弗里德曼将此时的失业率称作"自然失业率"，并假定其大致保持稳定。[3]

对于上述分析，弗里德曼总结道："（货币当局）无法通过控制名义值来盯住实际值，如实际利率、实际失业率、实际国民收入水平、实际货币数量、实际国民收入增长率，或者实际货币数量增长率。"[4]换言之，弗里德曼表明，尽管菲利普斯曲线短期内可能有用，但长期来看则会出现反转，因此，依据该曲线来制定政策并非明智之举。

尽管弗里德曼在论文中用了大量篇幅论述货币政策的局限性，但在结论中，他仍然为政策制定者可以怎样以及应该怎样行动提出了若干建议。最为重要的是他建议道：货币政策的目标应该是为经济提供稳定的货币基础，以便管理预期，避免意外冲击。具体而言，这意味着"公开将实现特定货币总量的稳定增长率作为政策目标"。[5]换言之，弗里德曼对于一个经济体的货币供应（可供使用的货币数量）的实际水平并不太关心。他所关心的是：货币供应应该保持恒定的增速，且货币供应的增加应该是公开透明的。[6]

随着弗里德曼上述论文的发表，在长达十几年的时间内，保持货币供应的稳定增长成为货币政策的核心原则。

《货币政策的作用》的学术价值

尽管只有 17 页，《货币政策的作用》却是经济学的一篇核心文献。该文为宏观经济学领域广泛采用的货币主义观点奠定了理论基础，其影响一直持续至今。但是，该文也成功预测了多个经济问题并一一应验。正如弗里德曼本人所说，"毫无疑问"，该文的广泛影响得益于其成功预测了 20 世纪 70 年代拖累西方经济的若干经济问题。[7] 正因如此，该文被公认是 20 世纪最伟大的经济学家之一所撰写的最具影响力的论文之一。

阅读该文，即可直击货币政策的核心问题：调整货币供应规模有何作用？有效性如何？最有用的货币政策目标是什么？

尽管弗里德曼对上述问题的部分解答在今天看来已不再正确，追寻他的思路却仍有价值。重要的是学会思考一些问题，如货币供应的变化会如何引起就业与物价水平的改变？通过这些思考，我们就能更加深入地了解时事，比如，围绕美国中央银行即美国联邦储备系统 * 及其对于 2008 至 2010 年金融危机的应对方式所产生的种种甚嚣尘上的争议。那么，货币政策是否能够有效地帮助经济恢复健康，尤其是在经济深陷危机之时？围绕这一问题产生了诸多意见分歧，而这正是弗里德曼的论文所研究的问题。[8]

除了在具体的经济学问题上的贡献，弗里德曼的论文也是逻辑推理的典范。通过研读该文，不同学术专业的学生都能获益匪浅，他们会学到，对于一个广为接受但可能存在误导的观念如何进行分解。该文中，弗里德曼沿用了自己在其他论文中的常用方法，即将学术对手的每个观点推导至逻辑终点。在该文中，他首先描述了菲

6

利普斯曲线在短期内可能适用，但紧接着就表明曲线的效果最终会被回调。这种论证方式会促使读者对自己已有的思想观念产生质疑，并由此获得成长、进步的机会。

1. 米尔顿·弗里德曼："自传"，《诺贝尔经济学奖》，登录日期2013年5月12日，http://www.nobelprize.org/nobel_prizes/economics/laureates/1976/friedman-autobio.html。

2. 娜奥米·克莱因：《休克主义：灾难资本主义的兴起》，多伦多：加拿大克诺夫出版集团，2009年。

3. 米尔顿·弗里德曼："货币政策的作用"，《美国经济评论》第58卷，1968年3月1日第1期，第8页。

4. 弗里德曼："货币政策的作用"，第11页。

5. 弗里德曼："货币政策的作用"，第16页。

6. 弗里德曼："货币政策的作用"，第17页。

7. 摘自布莱恩·斯诺登和霍华德·R.文：《现代宏观经济学：起源、发展与现状》，切尔滕纳姆：爱德华·埃尔加出版社，2005年，第204页。

8. 斯蒂芬·威廉森："柯薛拉柯塔之谜"，登录日期2015年2月18日，http://newmonetarism.blogspot.com/2013/09/kocherlakota-puzzle.html。

第一部分：学术渊源

1 作者生平与历史背景

要 点 ⚷

- 《货币政策的作用》一文研究了对于政策制定者至关重要的一个问题：如果可以的话，政府——更确切地说，政府的货币政策——在经济管理中应该发挥何种作用？

- 在大萧条中的成长经历给弗里德曼打下了深深的烙印。他批判了凯恩斯主义对于大萧条的分析。在他看来，糟糕的货币政策导致了经济的崩溃。

- 该文写于第二次世界大战（World War Ⅱ）*之后，当时，经济政策广受争议。有人沿袭凯恩斯主义传统，主张实行中央计划经济以及强力的政府干预；其他人则主张奉行古典主义经济学传统*，尽量减少政府干预。

为何要读这篇文章？

米尔顿·弗里德曼的论文《货币政策的作用》为研究整体经济的宏观经济学*做出了关键性贡献，并在该领域简洁、清晰地表达了货币主义的立场。

货币主义产生于 20 世纪中叶，主要由弗里德曼领导创立。该理论反对当时的主流观点，即认为政府可以通过调整国家货币供应规模来改善经济。该主流观点受到了英国著名经济学家约翰·梅纳德·凯恩斯的追随者的大力追捧。

货币主义认为，上述做法短期内或许有效，但长期来看，包括增加就业在内的所有积极效果都会消失殆尽，因此只会弊大于利。在货币主义者看来，政府的首要任务是调整货币供应*以保持物价稳定。

该论文原本是 1967 年为了在美国经济协会做演讲而写的讲稿，它迅即对经济学家在货币政策方面的态度产生了深刻的影响。本次演讲和随后撰写的论文使得经济学家和政策制定者的主流经济观点从凯恩斯主义转向货币主义，并使货币主义在 20 世纪 70 年代大行其道。这种影响力在同类作品中是不多见的。

弗里德曼的目标是向人们阐明在他的理解中什么才是有助于实现经济稳定的有效的货币政策。他认为，稳定意味着"高就业、物价稳定和高增长。"[1] 演讲的标题清晰易懂。《货币政策的作用》提出，货币政策对于经济政策的制定至关重要，但人们对于其作用和机制却存在广泛的误解。具体而言，弗里德曼认为，20 世纪五六十年代的凯恩斯主义经济学家们误解了通货膨胀与失业之间的关系，错误地认为政府可以通过放任通货膨胀来减少失业。这种误解源自于人们对于菲利普斯曲线所做的分析。该曲线显示，上述两个变量之间存在统计上的负相关。换言之，根据该曲线，如果放任通货膨胀升高，将有助于减少失业。弗里德曼运用精确的逻辑表明，这种关联的确有效，但只是短期的，长期来看必将失效。

> "弗里德曼总说，自己和同事对于古典主义经济学理论与实践的复兴所做的最大贡献，不在于他们多么善于宣传自己的观点，而在于他们的学术热情和专业能力。在经济学领域，即使是对弗里德曼的经济政策偏好提出尖锐批评意见的人，也对他的杰出才华和学术造诣深表认同。"
>
> ——兰尼·埃宾斯坦：《米尔顿·弗里德曼传》评论

作者生平

1912 年，米尔顿·弗里德曼出生于美国纽约市的一个东欧犹太移民家庭。[2] 在他的描述中，他的家庭"收入微薄，对外面的世界不甚了解。"[3] 他的童年和成年生活早期正值"大萧条"时期，他在此期间所经历的经济上的不确定性，很可能对他日后的经济学观点产生了影响。尤其是他在青少年时期就产生了一种强烈信仰，笃信"进取心、创新、创造、勤奋与节俭等这些最基本的力量才是实现经济增长的真正源泉。"[4]

尽管上述理念在弗里德曼的其他著作中表现得更为显著，但它仍有助于我们理解《货币政策的作用》一文。弗里德曼之所以会对当时人们普遍接受的凯恩斯主义货币政策发起挑战，在一定程度上是为了呼吁政府在改善经济的能力方面必须保持谦卑。

1932 年，弗里德曼毕业于新泽西州罗格斯大学数学专业，随后获得两个研究生课程的奖学金机会：一个是在布朗大学做数学研究，另一个是在芝加哥大学做经济学研究。他选择了后者，据他后来回忆，原因是大萧条让他觉得经济学是更为重要的研究领域。1933 年，他获得了芝加哥大学的经济学硕士学位。1946 年，他又获得位于纽约的哥伦比亚大学的博士学位。随后他返回芝加哥大学任教，直至 1977 年退休。[5] 退休后，他仍然活跃于公共政策领域，直至 2006 年逝世。

在弗里德曼的整个职业生涯中，无论是在学术界还是在公开辩论中，他都热衷于挑战人们普遍接受的主流观点。他始终活跃于公众的视野中。例如，他与经济学家安娜·施瓦茨＊合著并广为引用的著作《美国货币史》，就直接批评了人们对于大萧条产生原因的普遍看法，尤其是弗里德曼在书中驳斥了认为货币政策与大萧条无关的观点。[6]

弗里德曼的上述批评影响巨大，以至于 2002 年负责监管美国中央银行的美国联邦储备委员会 *7 名委员之一的本·伯南克 * 公开宣布，"关于大萧条的起因，您是对的，是我们做错了，我们很抱歉。但是，多亏有您，我们不会重蹈覆辙了。"[7]

创作背景

大萧条是 20 世纪的关键性经济事件，对于日后的经济思维与政策的发展起到了至关重要的作用。自 1929 年股票市场 * 崩盘，直至第二次世界大战爆发，大萧条使得美国经济急剧萎缩，并对全世界产生了深远的影响。"大萧条实验室"正是凯恩斯主义的许多核心思想的诞生之所，20 世纪绝大多数的宏观经济学家都在致力于研究大萧条的应对之道。1995 年，伯南克写道："理解大萧条是宏观经济学的圣杯。"[8]

对于弗里德曼而言，大萧条的影响既是学术的，也是个人的。他的早年生活受到了大萧条时期经济动荡的影响，他的学术研究也是在经济不安全的环境中进行的。弗里德曼写道："我理所当然地就认为，我要上大学，尽管同时我也认为，我需要自己承担所有费用。当时，我获得了一份可以上罗格斯大学的大额奖学金……我1932 年从罗格斯大学毕业，便开始从事各种兼职，以便为随后的深造筹集学费。我当过餐厅服务员、零售店店员，偶尔也做些创业投资，还打过暑期零工。"[9] 正是在这场经济灾难的大背景下，弗里德曼在 1932 年开始学术生涯之初就确信，个人的主动性比任何其他来源的经济支持都重要。这一态度在其《货币政策的作用》一文中随处可见。

1. 米尔顿·弗里德曼："货币政策的作用",《美国经济评论》第58卷,1968年3月1日第1期,第1页。

2. 蓝尼·艾伯斯坦:《米尔顿·弗里德曼传》,贝辛斯托克:帕尔格雷夫出版社,2007年,第5—12页。

3. 布赖恩·斯诺登和霍华德·R. 文:《现代宏观经济学:起源、发展与现状》,切尔滕纳姆:爱德华·埃尔加出版社,2005年,第199页。

4. 弗里德曼："货币政策的作用",第17页。

5. 斯诺登和文:《现代宏观经济学:起源、发展与现状》,第198—199页。

6. 米尔顿·弗里德曼和安娜·施瓦茨:《美国货币史(1867—1960)》,新泽西州普林斯顿:普林斯顿大学出版社,1963年。

7. 本·伯南克："致辞",登录日期2015年2月18日,http://www.federalreserve.gov/boarddocs/Speeches/2002/20021108/default.htm。

8. 本·伯南克："大萧条的宏观经济学比较研究",《信用、货币与金融》第27卷,1995年2月第1期,第1页。

9. 米尔顿·弗里德曼："自传",《诺贝尔经济学奖》,登录日期2013年5月12日,http://www.nobelprize.org/nobel_prizes/economics/laureates/1976/friedman-autobio.html。

2 学术背景

要点 ⌐o┉

- 经济学研究总体上分为两部分：研究个人和公司的微观经济学*以及研究整体国民经济的宏观经济学。弗里德曼的著作属于后者。

- 自 20 世纪 30 年代的凯恩斯主义革命和第二次世界大战以来，世界各国政府和央行都一致从古典经济学（即认为经济具有自我调节能力的理论）转向更加积极的经济管理政策。

- 弗里德曼属于古典经济学阵营，摒弃政府干预的理论，支持自由市场*资本主义*。

著作语境

米尔顿·弗里德曼的论文《货币政策的作用》讨论的是经济学，即研究社会商品生产、流通与消费*的理论。

英国经济学家莱昂内尔·罗宾斯*曾给经济学下了一条著名的定义：经济学是"把人类行为当作特定目的与具有各种不同用途的稀缺手段之间的关系来研究的科学"。[1] 尽管罗宾斯的定义强调了经济学中稀缺性*的重要性，但并未充分展示经济学概念的广度。经济学总体上分为两个组成部分：微观经济学与宏观经济学。

微观经济学研究个人与公司层面的经济生活。它的研究问题包括个人如何做出消费决定以及公司如何设定价格等。宏观经济学研究整体经济，这正是《货币政策的作用》一文的研究内容。

宏观经济学家不关注经济中的具体公司或个人，而是研究国家、地区乃至全球层面的经济生活。为此，他们需要使用一些经济指标*与其他变量，如：国民生产总值*（即在特定时间内一国境内所有商品与服务的总价值，有时候被称为"国内生产总值"）、失业率、汇率*、增长率*、利率，以及价格水平*等。

值得注意的是，上述指标都是国家与地区变量，而罗宾斯的定义强调的是个人在经济中的作用。例如，利率的改变可能会使个人行为发生改变，但宏观经济学家只对能在更高层面发挥作用的行为变化感兴趣。

> "如果财政部在旧瓶子里塞满钞票，再把瓶子埋起来……然后再让私营企业在久经考验的自由放任*原则下把钞票挖出来……那就不会再有失业问题了。"
>
> —— 约翰·梅纳德·凯恩斯：《就业、利息与货币通论》

学科概览

现代经济学可以追溯到苏格兰政治经济学家亚当·斯密*及其著作《国富论》（1776）。[2] 该书所呈现的资本主义模型直到今天仍有意义。

《国富论》主要论述自由市场。在该书创作时，"重商主义"*经济政策（禁止跨国贸易）正大行其道。书中，亚当·斯密创立了一套清晰的理论，表明自由贸易*和劳动分工*（国内与国际都适用）如何能够造福社会。

亚当·斯密认为，市场是人类生活中的自然存在。他相信，人们都愿意为了交换物品而进行货运、易物或贸易；换言之，都愿意在市场上自由交易商品，这种意愿是普遍存在的。[3] 或许最为重要的是，在亚当·斯密描绘的经济中，个人在直接追求私利时，却为社会带来了最好的结果。他最为著名的概念"看不见的手"表达了这一思想：当个人做出决定追求个人利益最大化时，市场的力量，即他所说的"看不见的手"，会引导这些个人决定，共同实现最佳社会结果。[4] 亚当·斯密写道：对于任何不知名的经济参与者（即在任何层面参与经济的任何人）而言，"通过追求个人利益，他往往促进了社会利益，效果甚至好于他真想促进社会利益时所能达到的程度。"[5]

虽然亚当·斯密被认为是自由市场的支持者，但是他的许多著名的追随者对于自由市场却持批判的态度。例如，卡尔·马克思 * 的著作《资本论》（1867）就对自由市场资本主义进行了强烈的批判，因为他相信市场会导致财富集中到资本家手中。[6] 马克思写道："在资本主义制度下，提高社会劳动生产率的所有方法的出现，都是以牺牲劳工的利益为代价的。"[7]

亚当·斯密认为，市场在一定程度上是可以自我纠正的。但是马克思却认为，市场是在资本拥有者与赚取工资者之间制造不平等的幕后推手。

经济学领域的另一关键性著作就是约翰·梅纳德·凯恩斯的《就业、利息与货币通论》（1936）。该书为政府实施干预以刺激经济提供了新的支持。凯恩斯理论的一个核心思想就是总需求 *，即对经济体中商品和服务的总需求。或者，正如凯恩斯所说，那是一种经济力量，该力量"将各种假设就业量与其总产出的预期收益联系起来。"[8]

这种模糊表述是凯恩斯有意为之。凯恩斯主义者相信，总需求可能会"受到许多公共和私人经济决定的影响，有时甚至毫无规律"[9]，即指在一定程度上是随机的。

凯恩斯主义者也相信，当需求下降、带来衰退威胁时，政府通过财政刺激*实施干预，增加政府在公路、教育、军队等方面的支出，能够帮助经济恢复生产能力。

学术渊源

弗里德曼的论文《货币政策的作用》并非是在学术真空中完成的，而是与芝加哥经济学派有着广泛的联系。该学派的主导思想就是价格理论。该理论的基本观点是，自由市场中商品或服务的价值是由供求关系决定的，并通过价格反映出来。一个简单的例子就是有关水和钻石的悖论。

水有着巨大的经济价值——生命离不开水。但是，钻石却被认为是奢侈品，而并非必需品。悖论就是，更加重要的商品——水，其经济价值反而低许多。价格理论可以通过稀缺性原则解释这一悖论。价格是由对商品的需求与其稀缺性之间的关系所决定的：水虽有价值但不稀缺，所以价格远低于钻石。

在许多方面，尤其是在对价格具有自我调节能力的观点上，芝加哥学派的价格理论可回溯到古典主义经济学传统，该传统在马克思和凯恩斯提出批判之前占据主流。

弗里德曼的著作也吸收了经济学家克努特·维克塞尔*与欧文·费舍尔*的思想。他们是名义与真实利率思想的主要提出者。弗里德曼写道："感谢维克塞尔，是他让我们了解到'自然'利率的概念，以及'自然'与'市场'利率之间存在差异的可能。"[10]在此基础上，费舍尔又补充了真实与名义利率的差异。[11]

费舍尔强调了价格变化预期的重要性，此观点被弗里德曼用作《货币政策的作用》一文中的一个核心思想："经验显示，利率很少能对价格水平的变化做出完美的自我调节，因为价格变化不能完全预期。"[12]

1. 莱昂内尔·罗宾斯：《论经济学的性质与意义》，伦敦：麦克米伦出版社，1932年，第 15 页。

2. 亚当·斯密：《国富论（精选本）》，牛津：牛津大学出版社，1998 年。

3. 斯密：《国富论》，第 62 页。

4. 斯密：《国富论》，第 14 页。

5. 斯密：《国富论》，第 14 页。

6. 卡尔·马克思：《资本论》，弗里德里希·恩格斯编，纽约：科西莫出版社，2007 年。

7. 马克思：《资本论》，第 708 页。

8. 约翰·梅纳德·凯恩斯：《就业、利息与货币通论》，登录日期 2015 年 2 月 18 日，http://cas.umkc.edu/economics/people/facultypages/kregel/courses/econ645/winter2011/generaltheory.pdf。

9. 艾伦·布林德："凯恩斯主义经济学"，经济学与自由图书馆，登录日期 2015 年 2 月 18 日，http://www.econlib.org/library/Enc/KeynesianEconomics.html。

10. 弗里德曼："货币政策的作用"，第 7 页。

11. 欧文·费舍尔：《货币的购买力》，纽约：科西莫出版社，2006 年。

12. 费舍尔：《货币的购买力》，第 210 页。

3 主导命题

要点 ⚷

- 尽管弗里德曼希望减少政府对经济的干预，但他同时也支持政府相关机构发挥一项特定职能：由中央银行对货币供应实施审慎管理。

- 弗里德曼的论文是对美国中央银行即美国联邦储备系统以往五十年工作的回应。过去五十年中，有两种政策手段，即重在调节货币供应的货币政策与重在调节政府支出的财政政策＊，交替成为提振经济的最佳手段。

- 弗里德曼认为，政府过于迷信通过调节经济中的货币供应就能管控经济增长与失业等宏观经济指标。

核心问题

在米尔顿·弗里德曼的论文标题"货币政策的作用"中，"作用"一词指的是货币政策在宏观经济管理与政策制定中所应当扮演的角色。

"货币政策"指的是政府对于货币供应的调节，即回收流通中的货币，或者印制更多钞票。具体而言，弗里德曼想要在"强调货币政策局限"的同时，"尝试厘清货币政策的功能以及如何利用货币政策才能最好地促进"宏观经济管理。[1] 他想向人们展示一种新的思想：真正有效的货币政策能够有助于实现如下具体目标，即"高就业、物价稳定和高增长"。[2]

然而，与此同时，弗里德曼的真正意图是：向同时代的经济共识（或者说，最主流意见）发起挑战。弗里德曼认为，在货币政策领域，政府对经济实施了过多的控制。他想要减少政府的经济干预，并希望说服经济学家和政策制定者接受他所提出的有限货币政策的建议。他写道："我们现在面临一种风险，即赋予了货币政策超出其能力的过大的职能，要求它实现（但结果却妨碍原本可以实现的）对经济的贡献"。[3]

> "人们普遍同意，经济政策的主要目标是：高就业、物价稳定和高增长。但是，对于这些目标是否能够彼此兼顾，人们的意见就不那么一致了。或者说，在那些认为这些目标不能兼顾的人之中，最大的分歧就在于，为了实现这些目标，各种政策工具能够并且应该发挥怎样的作用。"
>
> —— 米尔顿·弗里德曼：《货币政策的作用》

参与者

弗里德曼的论文是对此前五十年货币政策历史的回应。美国的中央银行，即美国联邦储备系统*，简称"美联储"，成立于1913年，旨在调节美国货币政策。美联储被赋予的政策目标是"营造易商环境"并且管理"经济总体信用情况。"[4]自美联储创立以来，经济学家和政策制定者对其确切作用的看法却在不断变化。

20世纪20年代早期，美联储广受赞誉，因为它具有对经济"进行微调的能力"，并被认为成功缔造了这一时期的"相对稳定"。[5]即使是在1929年的金融危机和随后的大萧条之后，许多观察家都认为美联储对于经济复苏至关重要。比如，1932年，政治家阿道夫·萨巴斯说道："我坚信，美国联邦储备委员会有能力缓解金融和商业困境。"他所指的是由大萧条引起的需求的急剧下降。

直到此时，人们还是普遍相信，货币政策（即调节货币供应）可以对就业和增长产生重大影响。但是，20 世纪 30 年代约翰·梅纳德·凯恩斯的著作出版之后，上述信念的吸引力大为减弱。总体而言，凯恩斯支持财政干预（即政府支出），而非货币政策行动。比如，1934 年，他写道："很难仅仅通过操纵货币就实现商业扩张。但是，（政府直接开支）远比这个重要，并且我认为也会带来更大希望。"[6]

20 世纪 50 年代，货币政策重获声誉，重新被人们看作重要的政策工具，这主要归功于发现了菲利普斯曲线。该曲线以经济学家威廉·菲利普斯命名。根据该曲线可知，通货膨胀*与失业之间存在负相关：换言之，放任通货膨胀会降低失业率；相反，压制通货膨胀却会引发更多的失业。[7] 对此，菲利普斯得出结论，"统计证据总体上支持如下假设：……货币工资率的变化率（通货膨胀的一种定义方式），可以通过失业水平以及失业变化率来解释。"[8]

尽管菲利普斯的发现似乎显示通货膨胀与失业之间存在一种很强的相关性，但是，直到 1960 年，美国经济学家才开始将菲利普斯曲线看作一项有效的政策工具。

那一年，经济学家保罗·萨缪尔森和罗伯特·索洛*共同发表了一篇预测美国菲利普斯曲线的论文。他们的结论是，物价保持每年百分之四到五的增长，"似乎将是最近若干年维持高就业率和高生产率的必要成本。"[9]

尽管萨缪尔森和索洛对于菲利普斯曲线的长期可靠性持怀疑态度，但是他们的论文被普遍认为支持货币政策可以用于失业目标调控的观点。[10] 这是因为，增加货币供应就会导致通货膨胀率升高，而限制货币供应则会抑制物价上涨。

当代论战

据说，当弗里德曼写作《货币政策的作用》时，凯恩斯的主张虽仍广为接受，但也已准备迎接批评。1970 年，在谈及菲利普斯曲线的问题时，经济学家哈里·约翰逊 * 写道：凯恩斯的主张"与其所批评的正统经济学理论有着同样的重大缺陷，即试图用真正的理论混合临时理论（即匆忙提出的理论）的方法来解释本质上属于货币现象的问题"。[11] 从这个意义上讲，弗里德曼的"货币政策的作用"立论正合时宜，发表时机也正当其时，读者很乐意接受他的观点。

弗里德曼非常熟悉美国货币政策的历史，熟悉学术界对于货币的经济作用的态度的转变。他 1963 年的著作《美国货币史》在包含丰富历史故事的同时，也非常重视人们对于货币政策导向的争论。[12] 因此，作为他论文的灵感来源，他在美国经济协会所做的演讲就是对当时的普遍观念发出的明确批判。

论文的读者不必阅读历史文献原文，就能了解这段历史，这要归功于弗里德曼在文中所做的总结。但是，如果了解已有普遍观点的发展脉络，对于理解弗里德曼的写作意图还是有帮助的。弗里德曼并没有明确点出批判对象的具体名称，而只是提及"当下流行的观点"。[13] 但是，鉴于他发表演讲的时代背景，应该说，弗里德曼的读者是非常清楚他心中的批判对象到底为何的。

1. 米尔顿·弗里德曼："货币政策的作用"，《美国经济评论》第 58 卷，1968 年 3 月 1 日第 1 期，第 5 页。

2. 弗里德曼："货币政策的作用"，第 1 页。

3. 弗里德曼："货币政策的作用"，第 5 页。

4. "1913 年联邦储备法"，登录日期 2015 年 2 月 18 日，http://legisworks.org/sal/38/stats/STATUTE-38-Pg251a.pdf。

5. 弗里德曼："货币政策的作用"，第 1 页。

6. 摘自米尔顿·弗里德曼和安娜·施瓦茨：《美国货币史（1867—1960）》，新泽西州普林斯顿：普林斯顿大学出版社，1963 年，第 409 页。

7. 阿尔班·菲利普斯："英国货币工资率变化率与失业的关系（1861—1957）"，《经济学刊》第 25 卷，1958 年第 100 期，第 283—299 页。

8. 菲利普斯："英国货币工资率变化率与失业的关系（1861—1957）"，第 299 页。

9. 保罗·萨缪尔森和罗伯特·索洛："抑制通货膨胀政策分析"，《美国经济评论》第 50 卷，1960 年第 2 期，第 192 页。

10. 保罗·克鲁格曼："庇古效应"，登录日期 2015 年 2 月 18 日，http://krugman.blogs.nytimes.com/2013/08/10/the-pigou-effect-double-super-special-wonkish/。

11. 哈里·约翰逊："凯恩斯主义革命和货币主义的反向革命"，《美国经济评论》，第 61 卷，1971 年第 2 期，第 9 页。

12. 弗里德曼、施瓦茨：《美国货币史》。

13. 弗里德曼："货币政策的作用"，第 5 页。

4 作者贡献

要点 🔑

- 弗里德曼的办法很简单：如果政府想要积极地管理好经济，就应该大幅度减少货币政策的运用，而应当追求稳定且可预期的货币政策。

- 弗里德曼的论文是对过去几十年经济学正统观念的批判。正统观念认为，市场（如劳动力市场和商品价格）存在缺陷，需要积极有力的政府干预。

- 弗里德曼的观点与另一位经济学家埃德蒙·费尔普斯*十分接近。他们两位都拒绝接受当时的普遍观点，即故意放任通货膨胀能拉低失业，反之亦然。

作者目标

在论文《货币政策的作用》中，米尔顿·弗里德曼提出，经济学家萨缪尔森和索洛对于菲利普斯曲线的解释存在谬误，原因有二。首先，该解释未能说明名义价值与实际价值之间的区别。（实际价值要依据通货膨胀进行调整。如果你的名义工资上涨 2%，而通货膨胀率是 5%，那么，你的实际工资就会下降 3%。）其次，该解释在做出长期预测时，并未考虑人们对于经济的预期。

弗里德曼并不是第一个提出这些思想的人。例如，奥地利裔美国经济学家戈特弗里德·哈伯勒*在 1960 年的时候就指出了预期的作用："随着日益蔓延的通货膨胀的持续，越来越多的人将会预期价格进一步上涨，并且会采取措施保护自己……工会也会要求大幅加薪，以确保取得实际的生活改善。"[1] 弗里德曼的原创性在于其论点清晰完整、合乎逻辑。

该论文围绕三部分展开。

首先，弗里德曼简要回顾了 20 世纪初以来美国政府和央行的政策演变，并在此过程中提出了自己对于这些政策变化的分析。论文的这一部分得到他自己先前货币经济学著作的支持，尤其是他 1963 年的著作《美国货币史》。该书有时仅仅被他称作"最近的研究"。[2]

然后，他继而讨论自己的核心目标。这里，他的重点是他认为货币政策无效的两个方面，即设定不同国家货币间的汇率以及降低失业率。

最后，他提出了自己对于"货币政策应当怎样实施"的观点。弗里德曼观点的一个核心部分就是他对于自由企业和个人责任的一种广为人知的信念。在论文末尾，他写道："稳定的货币增长会提供一种有利的货币环境，这将有助于有效运用一些基本的力量，比如进取心、创新、创造、勤奋和节俭，而这些正是实现经济增长的真正的源泉。根据我们目前的知识水平，这是我们能够对货币政策抱有的最高期待。但是，这种期待本身已经非常了不起，显然也是我们有能力达到的。"[3]

> "显而易见，（该文是）战后最具影响力的宏观经济学论文。"
>
> —— 罗伯特·斯基德尔斯基：评《货币政策的作用》

研究方法

就像弗里德曼大多数的学术著作一样，在许多方面，《货币政策的作用》一文也参考了古典主义经济学传统＊。根据该传统，经济是可以进行自我调节的。在弗里德曼看来，与约翰·梅纳德·凯恩斯的追随者密切相关的政府所奉行的积极财政政策背叛了古典主义经济学原则。他希望能够采取一种以价格为基础的方式，将古典主义思想重新引入经济学。

第二次世界大战以来，凯恩斯学派的思想在学术界和政策圈里一直都是经济管理的主要方式。因此，弗里德曼在1965年做出了著名的论断："我们现在都是凯恩斯主义者"。[4]

弗里德曼说这句话时的意思并不能完全从字面上理解。他解释道：这是对凯恩斯主义研究方法的采纳，而不是对凯恩斯主义理论的采纳。他写道："我们都使用凯恩斯主义的语言和研究方法"。他指的是凯恩斯使用总值（即能够反映经济运行效益的"宏观总量"）来分析经济的方式。

但是，无论弗里德曼如何看待凯恩斯主义的分析方法，他清楚地表明，自己并不接受"凯恩斯主义的主要结论。"[5] 具体而言，弗里德曼拒绝接受如下观点，即货币供应量的变化，或者任何其他的政府干预，能够改变市场上失业率的"自然"水平。在此方面，弗里德曼受到价格理论的启发。

根据价格理论，商品和劳动力的价格，而不是货币供应量规模等政府能够控制的其他因素，才是市场行为和实体经济的真正驱动力。

弗里德曼与凯恩斯的对立观点，被称作"货币主义"，其基础原则如下：

• 长期的货币中立性（该原则表明，长期来看，货币供应并不能够影响诸如失业等真实变量。）

- 短期的货币非中立性（该原则表明，短期来看，改变货币供应规模的确能够带来诸如减少失业等变化。）
- 承认实际利率与名义利率之间的差异
- 采用总体货币供应等措施作为分析的基础[6]

货币主义理论的一个重要方面，就是如下观点，即任何形式的价格控制（如最低工资）都会引起市场的扭曲。货币主义还认为，货币政策应当关注价格稳定，并应保持长期一致。[7]

时代贡献

尽管就许多方面而言，《货币政策的作用》是一篇原创论文，但是弗里德曼关于货币政策的诸多观点，与经济学家埃德蒙·费尔普斯在同一年也就是 1967 年发表的关于劳动力市场经济学的许多观点确有重合之处。[8]

弗里德曼和费尔普斯都认为，通货膨胀和失业之间并不存在长期的负相关。换言之，他们并不同意如下观点：故意放任更高的通货膨胀将会拉低失业率，反之亦然，尽管其被当时的经济学家所普遍接受，并已被菲利普斯曲线所"证明"。与弗里德曼的论文相比，费尔普斯的论文更加基于模型，但同时也是建立在承认实际工资和名义工资的区别以及预期思想的基础上的。费尔普斯写道：如果菲利普斯曲线背后的思想要被接受的话，"就必须加上预期通货膨胀率。"[9] 这是因为"工人们只会关注实际工资"。如果他们预期通货膨胀持续，就会要求更大幅度加薪，以弥补通货膨胀带来的损失，而不仅仅满足于购买力 * 的任何实际提升。因此，从长期来看，关于成本和工资的预期将会削弱菲利普斯曲线做出正确预测的能力。[10]

费尔普斯和弗里德曼两人有一个关键的共同点，就是他们都认为，长期来看，自然失业率不会因推高通货膨胀等政府行为而发生改变。

弗里德曼承认，他的论文与费尔普斯的分析之间的确存在"大量相似观点和许多重合之处"。主要的区别在于，弗里德曼是从货币政策和利率的角度来研究问题的，而费尔普斯的研究则是从劳动力市场动力学与工资方面着手的。但是他承认，他和费尔普斯的"理论是相同的"。[11]

---

1. 摘自詹姆斯·福德："弗里德曼—费尔普斯预期批评的历史地位"，《牛津经济学讨论论文系列》第 299 卷，2008 年 7 月，第 6 页。

2. 米尔顿·弗里德曼："货币政策的作用"，《美国经济评论》第 58 卷，1968 年 3 月 1 日第 1 期，第 3 页。

3. 弗里德曼："货币政策的作用"，第 17 页。

4. 米尔顿·弗里德曼："经济：我们现在都是凯恩斯主义者"，《时代》，1965 年 12 月 31 日。

5. 摘自罗杰·加里森："哈耶克与弗里德曼：针锋相对"，登录日期 2015 年 2 月 18 日，http://www.auburn.edu/~garriro/hayek%20and%20friedman.pdf。

6. 班尼特·麦卡勒姆："货币主义"，经济学与自由图书馆，登录日期 2015 年 2 月 18 日，http://www.econlib.org/library/Enc/Monetarism.html。

7. 麦卡勒姆："货币主义"。

8. 埃德蒙·费尔普斯："菲利普斯曲线，通货膨胀预期与长期最大就业"，《经济学刊》第 34 卷，1967 年第 135 期，第 254—281 页。

9. 费尔普斯："菲利普斯曲线"，第 261 页。

10. 凯文·胡佛："菲利普斯曲线"，登录时间 2015 年 2 月 18 日，http://www.econlib. org/library/Enc/PhillipsCurve.html。

11. 摘自布赖恩·斯诺登和霍华德·R. 文:《现代宏观经济学：起源、发展与现状》，切尔滕纳姆：爱德华·埃尔加出版社，2005 年，第 205 页。

第二部分：学术思想

5 思想主脉

要点 ⌐—ㅐ

- 在论文中，弗里德曼探讨了货币政策 * 理论的演变历史、货币政策作用的局限性以及应当适度实施货币政策的理论。

- 弗里德曼认为，政府对于货币政策期望过高。他说，长期来看，货币政策不能控制通货膨胀或者失业，强行这样使用货币政策最终只会损害经济增长。

- 论文的底稿是弗里德曼在美国经济协会的一次会议上的演讲稿。会上，他向与会同行专家陈述了他的观点。由于他认为听众都能理解他所谈论的问题，因此并未针对非专业人士做出解释。

核心主题

弗里德曼《货币政策的作用》一文的核心论题是政府如何利用货币政策来管理经济。这一问题可以归入凯恩斯主义 * 和古典主义 * 经济学家之间更为广泛的争论，他们对于政府干预在国民经济中的作用有严重分歧。弗里德曼对于这一问题的分析是围绕着几项经济指标 * 而展开的，包括货币供应 *、利率 *、失业和价格。

在弗里德曼撰写本论文的时候，政策制定者们普遍接受凯恩斯主义对于货币政策的观点，即支持利用政府能够控制的一切手段去管控经济、刺激需求，并且维持低失业率。弗里德曼试图证明，货币政策远没有凯恩斯主义政策制定者们所想象的那般有效，并且实际上可能已经对经济稳定造成了损害。

在这个核心主题之下，弗里德曼的论文还包含几个分主题。

首先，就是货币政策的历史演变，以及从 20 世纪 20 年代到 20 世纪 60 年代晚期人们对于货币政策的不同见解。让弗里德曼尤为感兴趣的是，对于货币政策是否能够在通货膨胀和失业控制方面达到某些具体效果，人们的态度发生了数次变化。

20 世纪 20 年代，货币政策曾被认为是极为有效的。当时，人们普遍相信，新的时代已经来临，货币技术[1]已经使商业周期*理论显得过时（换言之，对货币供应的管理将会消除经济的大起大落）。然而，在大萧条之后，"人们的观念又转向了另一个极端"，货币政策被认为几乎完全无力应对经济危机。[2]

在 20 世纪五六十年代，主流观点再次发生转变，货币政策又被认为是管理经济结果的有效方式。正如弗里德曼所说，"今天，货币政策被赋予的首要任务，就是促进全面就业。防止通货膨胀虽然仍然受到持续关注，但无疑已是次要关切。"[3]

弗里德曼也在论文中探讨了货币政策的局限性，并且重点论述了在他看来货币政策无效的两个领域，即设定利率以及"在超出极为有限的时间范围内"降低失业。[4]利率和失业是宏观经济的核心问题。因此，通过表明货币政策在这两个领域内收效甚微，弗里德曼事实上是做出了一个极为强大的论断。

最后，弗里德曼讨论了"应当如何实施货币政策"。他在文中列举了自己的政策偏好，即在货币政策允许的范围内，中央银行应当如何行事，才能维持经济的健康。[5]

弗里德曼的核心主题和分主题以一种符合逻辑而又清晰的方式呈现出来，最终得出如下结论：政府政策的真正目标，应当是促进自由企业的发展，而不是管理诸如失业和通货膨胀等指标。

> "因此，首要一点，我要强调有哪些事情是货币政策无法做到的。然后，基于我们目前已知和未知的知识，我再继续描述它能做到的事情，并说明怎样才能做出最大的贡献。"
>
> —— 米尔顿·弗里德曼：《货币政策的作用》

思想探究

弗里德曼在《货币政策的作用》一文中的主要思想是：货币政策并非实现长期通货膨胀目标或失业目标的有效工具。相反，货币政策的目标应当是"避免犯错"，并"为经济提供一个稳定的环境"。[6] 具体而言，弗里德曼认为，货币政策的制定者应当尽力"公开采取货币政策，保持特定货币总量的稳定增长"。换言之，应当以一种恒定的、可预期的方式逐步增加货币供应。[7]

弗里德曼之所以建议政府货币政策的目标应仅限于保持货币总量的稳定增长，是因为他对于货币政策能够实现更加具体的目标持怀疑态度。他写道："首要的要求是，货币当局应当以可控的而非不可控的政策强度（结果）为指引"。[8]

此外，他的写作动机还在于他对于大萧条（被他称作"大收缩"）起因的理解以及相信货币当局应当避免"货币政策的剧烈摇摆"。[9] 他写道："过去，货币当局偶尔会搞反货币政策的调控方向，大收缩时期就是这样。"[10]

这里，他指的是 1929 年金融危机爆发以后货币供应量的急剧减少。他继续写道："货币当局的调控方向在更多时候是正确的，尽管常常为时已晚，但却犯了调控幅度过大的错误。"[11]

弗里德曼认为，如果货币当局保持"货币供应量稳定且适度增长"，有助于宏观经济的稳定，并可"为避免通货膨胀或通货紧缩 *

做出重要贡献"。[12]

语言表述

由于《货币政策的作用》一文的底稿是为经济学家所做的演讲，语言风格就显得直接而又俏皮，并且假定听众对于货币政策的运作方式是有所了解的。弗里德曼的语气是专为经济学家而设计的，尤其是要说服经济学同行们他们通常的观点是错误的。弗里德曼频繁使用代词"你"来描述他的听众，这种文体风格通常不大会出现在学术论文当中，这使该论文显得更像是一篇非正式的研讨会报告，而非一篇学术论文。

读者如果想要轻松阅读该文，就需要事先了解一些宏观经济学术语与核心思想，比如失业、利率和汇率。此外，在阅读本文前，读者还需事先了解货币政策的普通知识，因为弗里德曼并未在文中提供相关定义或背景知识。

与许多经济学论文不同，《货币政策的作用》一文并没有使用数学。但是，它使用了非常严密的语言论证。对此，如果读者对于相关观点毫不熟悉的话，可能会觉得生涩难懂。例如，理解名义价值和实际价值之间的区别是理解弗里德曼论点的核心。但是，文中在论述这一区别之时，并未为读者提供任何关于这两个术语含义的总结。[13]

---

1. 米尔顿·弗里德曼："货币政策的作用"，《美国经济评论》第 58 卷，1968 年 3 月 1 日第 1 期，第 1 页。

2. 弗里德曼："货币政策的作用"，第1页。

3. 弗里德曼："货币政策的作用"，第5页。

4. 弗里德曼："货币政策的作用"，第5页。

5. 弗里德曼："货币政策的作用"，第14页。

6. 弗里德曼："货币政策的作用"，第12—13页。

7. 弗里德曼："货币政策的作用"，第16页。

8. 弗里德曼："货币政策的作用"，第14页。

9. 弗里德曼："货币政策的作用"，第15页。

10. 弗里德曼："货币政策的作用"，第15页。

11. 弗里德曼："货币政策的作用"，第16页。

12. 弗里德曼："货币政策的作用"，第17页。

13. 弗里德曼："货币政策的作用"，第8页。

6 思想支脉

要点 🔑

- 弗里德曼论文的思想支脉包括阐释菲利普斯曲线的缺陷，即该曲线忽略了名义工资和实际工资之间的区别。弗里德曼也考察了"自然失业率"，即从长期来看货币政策无法影响的一种失业率。
- 该论文举例说明增加货币供应的决定开始时刺激经济活动但是旧有平衡又很快重新建立起来的机制。
- 该论文更多地论述了弗里德曼在失业而非利率问题上的观点。

其他思想

弗里德曼的论文《货币政策的作用》中，最重要的思想支脉，就是他对于菲利普斯曲线的批评，这一批评支持了他对于总体而言被过份高估的货币政策的批判。

弗里德曼论点的核心是实际工资与名义工资之间的区别。名义工资是商品或服务标示的价格。因此，1960年，一名工人每小时赚7美元，就意味着他每小时的名义工资是7美元。但另一方面，他的实际工资却要因物价水平的历时变化而进行调整。因为物价水平的趋势是随通货膨胀而上涨，所以1960年的7美元工资会比如今工人所挣的7美元工资的价值要高，尽管两者的名义工资相同。换言之，我们要依据购买力来做出调整。所谓购买力，就是指在特定时期内特定数量的名义价值所能购买的商品和服务的数量。7美元在1960年的购买力远高于今天。因此，如果参照2015年的标准，1960年工人的实际工资将会远远高于7美元。

论文的另一重要观点就是"自然失业率",换言之,也就是当经济保持良好平衡时所呈现的失业率。[1] 对弗里德曼而言,至关重要的是自然失业率并不受货币因素的影响,而只与经济的结构特征相关,如原材料的供应价格是否合理,或者是否有足够的受过良好教育和培训的劳动力人口来完成经济体系中的所有工作。弗里德曼指出,自然失业率并非一成不变,而是事实上会随经济结构的改变而改变。例如,弗里德曼指出,"法定最低工资水平"的上涨以及"工会的强势"都将容易导致自然失业率的上涨,因为这些因素会增加企业雇佣新员工的成本。[2] 相反,"完善政府职业介绍机构"以及"提供更多的关于空余岗位和劳动力供应的信息"将有助于降低自然失业率。[3]

> "我担心,货币政策的钟摆已经偏离得太远,以至于我们实际上是在冒着巨大的风险,赋予货币政策其无力承担的责任,要求它完成其无法完成的任务,结果却很有可能妨碍其做出应有的贡献。"
>
> —— 米尔顿·弗里德曼:《货币政策的作用》

思想探究

弗里德曼赞扬菲利普斯曲线对于经济思想是一项"重要而且原创的贡献",但是却对其基本缺陷提出了挑战:该曲线未能区分名义工资和实际工资。[4] 尽管菲利普斯曲线显示,政策制定者可以通过调整货币供应来提高或者降低通货膨胀,进而达成控制失业率的目标,但是弗里德曼表明,这种影响只会短期有效,长期来看,对于通货膨胀的预期将会抵消短期内所达成的失业率控制目标。

　　为了说明其中的原因，弗里德曼提供了一个示例。首先，假定货币当局试图将失业率设定为3%，这一数值也假定低于自然失业率。[5]进一步假定，经济近期保持了物价水平平稳（也就是低通胀）和高于3%的顽固失业率。为了降低失业率，货币当局会提升货币供应量的增速。[6]向经济体系中注入现金将会增加支出；与此同时，更低的借贷成本也会刺激企业扩张经营。鉴于一个人的支出同时就是另一个人的收入，所以经济体系中的支出和收入都会上涨。

　　弗里德曼指出，这一增长的最初效果，会反映在生产和就业领域，而非物价水平上："面对需求的最初扩张，生产者会作出反应，加大生产；员工会工作更长的时间；失业者也会找到工作。这些新的工作机会，是在公司雇佣更多工人以满足已经增长的需求时产生的。"[7]因此，从短期来看，政策取得了预期的效果，经济体系中的现金注入增加了生产，降低了失业率。

　　但是，弗里德曼认为，这些只是"最初的效果"而已。[8]最终，货币政策的扩张将创造新的需求，商品销售的价格也会随之上涨。而这将会降低实际工资，毕竟实际工资是名义工资扣除物价因素以后的结果。

　　工资的增速通常慢于物价的上涨。因此，当商品和服务价格上涨时，工人的购买力将会下降。而当工人发现他们的实际工资下降时，他们会要求更高的名义工资。最终，失业率将回到自然失业率水平，因为雇主会因为需要支付新的更高的工资而裁员。为了能让货币当局实现3%的失业率控制目标，就需要进一步扩大货币供应，而这会提升通货膨胀。

　　弗里德曼认为，货币当局维持目标失业率的唯一的方法，就是

"使通货膨胀保持加速增长"，即不断提高通货膨胀水平。

对于利率，弗里德曼也表达了非常近似的观点。他表明，货币政策是无法长期维持目标利率的。[9]

被忽视之处

弗里德曼的论文底稿是对美国经济协会所做的演讲，该协会是美国最顶尖的经济学家行业组织。后来，该文发表在《美国经济评论》上，该杂志又是最重要的经济学刊物之一。自该论文发表以来，一开始便获得了人们的关注，此后的几十年中也得到了人们的持续关注，鉴于此，此论文没有任何细节被人们所忽略。而且，该论文的篇幅也很短，只有 17 页，这意味着那些了解该论文的评论家们已经仔细地研读了弗里德曼在其中所表达的所有思想。

该论文自 1968 年发表以来，当代宏观经济学的领军人物——从获得诺贝尔经济学奖的经济学家保罗·克鲁格曼*，到经济学家约翰·柯克伦*，都对它进行了分析和解读。[10] 对于该论文不同章节的兴趣几十年中此消彼长，但弗里德曼对于菲利普斯曲线的批评，以及他对于稳健货币政策的支持，始终位于人们讨论的前沿与核心。

该论文中有一个领域相对而言较少受到关注，即弗里德曼对于利率的讨论。正如弗里德曼对于菲利普斯曲线的批判性讨论，弗里德曼也认为货币政策不能够"超越极为有限的期限"而设定长期利率。[11] 利率问题之所以受到了较少的关注，很可能是因为无论是在论文发表之初，还是在出版以后引起的争论中，多数政策讨论的焦点都是就业，而非利率。

1. 米尔顿·弗里德曼："货币政策的作用",《美国经济评论》第 58 卷, 1968 年 3 月 1 日第 1 期, 第 7—8 页。

2. 弗里德曼："货币政策的作用", 第 9 页。

3. 弗里德曼："货币政策的作用", 第 9 页。

4. 弗里德曼："货币政策的作用", 第 8 页。

5. 弗里德曼："货币政策的作用", 第 9—10 页。

6. 弗里德曼："货币政策的作用", 第 9 页。

7. 弗里德曼："货币政策的作用", 第 10 页。

8. 弗里德曼："货币政策的作用", 第 10 页。

9. 弗里德曼："货币政策的作用", 第 5—6 页。

10. 保罗·克鲁格曼："米尔顿·弗里德曼是谁？", 登录日期 2015 年 2 月 18 日, http://www.nybooks.com/articles/archives/2007/feb/15/who-was-milton-friedman/; 约翰·柯克伦："再论货币政策的作用", 登录日期 2015 年 2 月 18 日, http://bfi.uchicago.edu/feature-story/role-monetary-policy-revisited。

11. 弗里德曼："货币政策的作用", 第 5 页。

7 历史成就

要点 ⚷

- 弗里德曼的论文影响巨大。即便是主要的左翼批评家也承认，弗里德曼成功指出了凯恩斯主义的核心弱点，尤其是他指出，通货膨胀和失业之间的替代关系只是临时的。

- 然而，当弗里德曼的货币主义经济学理论在 20 世纪 80 年代被美国和英国的右翼政府所奉行时，结果却是有好有坏。

- 尽管弗里德曼仍然受到自由主义者 * 的喜爱，但对于其他人而言，他与智利独裁者奥古斯托·皮诺切特 * 等右翼人物的关系，则对他的经济学遗产造成了损害。但是，即便他的批评者也承认，弗里德曼是一位伟大的经济学家。

观点评价

弗里德曼极其成功地达成了目标。他的论文《货币政策的作用》迅速对经济学行业产生了影响，即使是詹姆斯·托宾 * 等批评他的凯恩斯主义经济学家也难免受其影响。作为诺贝尔奖得主的经济学家保罗·克鲁格曼写道："弗里德曼对于凯恩斯的批评之所以会产生如此广泛的影响，就在于他正确地指出了凯恩斯主义的弱点。"[1]

瑞典经济学家埃里克·伦德伯格 * 于 1976 年为弗里德曼颁发诺贝尔经济学奖时说道："正是弗里德曼率先表明，人们普遍假定的在失业与通胀率之间存在的简单替代关系只是一种临时性现象。"[2] 弗里德曼的批评也产生了政治影响。例如，美国联邦储备委员会的几任主席面对弗里德曼的批评，都被迫为积极的货币政策做出辩护。1969 年，弗里德曼甚至呼吁美联储主席小威廉·麦克切斯尼·马丁*辞职。[3]

英国经济学家布赖恩·斯诺登和霍华德·R. 文写道："《美国货币史》无疑是弗里德曼最具影响力的专著，而《货币政策的作用》则毫无疑问是其最有影响力的论文。"1994 年，克鲁格曼说道："弗里德曼的论文是'战后最具决定性意义的学术成就之一'"。1996 年，罗伯特·斯基德尔斯基*写道："该文显然是战后发表的最具影响力的宏观经济学论文。"[4] 至今，《货币政策的作用》一文仍是经济学领域引用率最高的论文之一。与此同时，20 世纪 80 年代，美、英两国均寻求抑制通货膨胀，货币主义继而对两国的政策选择产生了强烈影响。在英国，该政策被称作"玛格丽特·撒切尔*首相的货币主义实验"。[5]

> "（该论文）很可能是经济学杂志历来刊发的论文中最具影响力的一篇。"
>
> —— 詹姆斯·托宾，经济学家，经常批判弗里德曼的学术观点

当时的成就

《货币政策的作用》一文也对全球公共政策产生了深刻影响。

2004 年，在就任美联储主席这一全球最具影响力的货币政策制定者职务之前，本·伯南克在一次著名的演讲中指出："在 20 世纪 60 年代末与 70 年代的大部分时间里，许多经济学家和政策制定者都认为，经济政策可以利用通货膨胀与失业之间永恒的替代关系，这种关系可以通过一条简单的菲利普斯曲线进行描述。存在这种永恒的替代关系的观点开启了一个充满诱惑力的前景，即只要允

许稍稍提高通货膨胀，政策制定者就可永久实现低失业率。当然，这种观点现在在理论与实践上均已遭到摒弃。"

伯南克指出，弗里德曼 1968 年的论文 "为这种永恒的替代关系提供了主要的理论批判"，虽然他同时也指出，"美国货币政策制定者究竟何时以及在多大程度上吸取了弗里德曼论文中所描述的教训，对此，学者们的意见尚有分歧。"[6]

弗里德曼的经济学观点付诸实施后的成效却是有好有坏。20 世纪 80 年代，英、美两国进行了货币主义实验，左翼政客普遍相信，这些实验导致了大规模失业，并且削弱了国家福利。此种情况在英国尤甚。非常重要的是，1980 年，在美国总统罗纳德·里根 * 竞选期间，弗里德曼继续担任非官方顾问。尽管弗里德曼的思想在经济学和公共政策领域中被广泛采用，但在更广阔的学术领域中，论文观点的应用却较为有限。

局限性

人们对于弗里德曼学术成就的评价，通常会受到对其自由主义政治观点的态度的影响。左翼政客尤其反对弗里德曼有关国家须尽量减少经济干预的观点。与此同时，人权主义者也强烈批评他在海外对自由市场思想的大力宣传，尤其是他在 20 世纪 70 年代中期担任了臭名昭著的智利皮诺切特政权的顾问，在此期间弗里德曼建议智利当局减少政府支出，以降低通货膨胀。[7]事实上，1976 年，左翼抗议者曾以人道主义为由，打断了授予弗里德曼诺贝尔经济学奖的颁奖仪式。

最近，加拿大作家娜奥米·克莱因 * 在其著作《休克学说》中，对弗里德曼提出了强烈的批评。针对弗里德曼对于私立教育的支持，克莱因写道："过去 30 多年中，弗里德曼和追随他的当权者们一直都在完善如下策略，即等到大的危机出现时，把部分国家资产出售给私营业主，而此时，普通百姓却仍在冲击中颤栗发抖。"[8]

与此同时，那些自由主义派政客们则倾向于把弗里德曼的著作看做是在谋求一个更加高效而自由社会的处方。当然，此时他们所参照的是弗里德曼的其他论文，而非《货币政策的作用》一文。另一方面，经济学家们则倾向于依据学术成就来评判弗里德曼的著作。比如，弗里德曼的著名批评者克鲁格曼就承认，弗里德曼是"一位伟大的经济学家和一个伟大的人"。[9]因此，基于不同的政治立场和职业背景，人们或许会对弗里德曼的著作作出不同的解读。

---

1. 保罗·克鲁格曼："米尔顿·弗里德曼是谁？"，登录日期 2015 年 2 月 18 日，http://www.nybooks.com/articles/archives/2007/feb/15/who-was-milton-friedman/。

2. 詹姆斯·福德："弗里德曼 — 费尔普斯预期批评的历史地位"，《牛津经济学讨论论文系列》第 299 卷，2008 年 7 月，第 2 页。

3. 爱德华·纳尔逊："米尔顿·弗里德曼与美国货币政策：1961—2006"，圣路易斯联邦储备银行工作文件系列，2007 年，登录日期 2015 年 2 月 18 日，http://research.stlouisfed.org/wp/2007/2007-002.pdf。

4. 布赖恩·斯诺登和霍华德·R. 文：《现代宏观经济学：起源、发展与现状》，切尔滕纳姆：爱德华·埃尔加出版社，2005 年，第 175 页。

5. 斯诺登和文：《现代宏观经济学：起源、发展与现状》，第 175 页。

6. 本·伯南克："大稳健"，2004 年 2 月 20 日在美国华盛顿特区"东部经济协会"上所作的报告，登录日期 2013 年 7 月 25 日，http://www.federalreserve.gov/

BOARDDOCS/SPEECHES/2004/20040220/default.htm。

7. 娜奥米·克莱因：《休克学说：灾难资本主义的兴起》，多伦多：加拿大克诺夫出版集团，2009 年。

8. 娜奥米·克莱因：《休克学说：灾难资本主义的兴起》，登陆日期 2015 年 2 月 18 日，http://www.naomiklein.org/shock-doctrine/excerpt。

9. 克鲁格曼："米尔顿·弗里德曼是谁？"。

8 著作地位

要点 🔑

- 弗里德曼在消费者选择 * 以及货币政策历史等众多经济学领域都做出了重要贡献，主要是对当时人们普遍接受的凯恩斯主义的观点进行了批判。

- 作为一名公共知识分子，弗里德曼为推动政府采取自由市场 * 政策进行了公开的斗争。

- 《货币政策的作用》一文代表了弗里德曼对全球货币政策制定所做出的最重要的贡献。该文与弗里德曼的大量其他著作一起，帮助他赢得了 1976 年的诺贝尔经济学奖。

定位

《货币政策的作用》一文写于 1967 年，正值弗里德曼学术创作能力的高峰期。在此之前，他曾就消费者选择、经济学方法论以及货币史等多个经济学专题撰写论文。在其职业生涯中，他也曾对经济学的诸多领域展开研究，但是，作为其理论出发点，他对于自由市场和自由企业的偏好却一直贯穿始终。

1957 年，弗里德曼撰写了《消费功能理论》一书。该书成为其早期知名著作之一。在书中，他介绍了持久收入假设 *：任何时期的消费（即在商品和服务方面的开支）都同时与个人的当前收入及预期未来收入相关。[1]

该假设对凯恩斯的观点提出了直接的挑战。凯恩斯认为，"个人和家庭会调整消费支出以反映其当前的收入水平"。[2] 换句话说，凯恩斯提出，个人每月的支出习惯，应当仅仅取决于其在特定月份中的收入水平。因此，如果他们在任何一个月中收入增加，那么他们的消费和储蓄模式也会随之改变。然而，在综合考虑"消费、财富和收入"[3]的基础上，弗里德曼的模型表明，个人当前的消费，应当由对其财富和收入的长期预期来说明。上述例子只是弗里德曼对于凯恩斯主义发出有力挑战的一个缩影。

1963 年，弗里德曼与经济学家安娜·施瓦茨合著的《美国货币史》一书，在很大程度上为《货币政策的作用》一文奠定了基础，该书的出版标志着人们对于大萧条（被弗里德曼称作"大收缩"）起因的理解发生了根本性的转变，同时也改变了货币政策的进程，迫使货币政策制定者认识到货币在宏观经济动力中的重要性。[4]

在谈及美国经济收缩时期货币储备（即流通中的货币总量）的急剧下降时，弗里德曼写道："如果没有货币储备的下降，那就无法想象货币收入和价格水平会在四年之内分别下降一半以上和三分之一以上。"[5]

在《美国货币史》出版以前，主流的观点与约翰·梅纳德·凯恩斯在《就业、利息和货币总论》中提出的观点有关，也就是：货币政策在经济危机中对于经济几乎没有影响。但是，弗里德曼的著作回顾了美国近 100 年的货币政策历史，旨在支持其观点，也就是：正是美联储限制流通中货币数量的决定，在很大程度上导致了大萧条的发生。

除了其在经济学领域开展的学术活动之外，弗里德曼作为公共知识分子也广受关注。他经常就教育、药品政策、外交政策等公共政策话题发表观点，并且几乎总在表达支持自由市场的立场。弗里德曼的知名度也源于其常就货币问题为外国政府提供咨询。例如，

1975 年，弗里德曼在写给智利总统奥古斯托·皮诺切特的一封信中，就建议其"大幅减缓货币总量的增速"，以避免快速的通货膨胀对经济造成损害。[6]

整合

弗里德曼是古往今来最伟大的经济思想家之一，他赢得这一声誉是实至名归的。《经济学人》杂志将弗里德曼描述为"20 世纪后半叶……也许是整个 20 世纪最有影响力的经济学家"。[7] 后来担任美联储主席的本·伯南克对弗里德曼的描述如下："弗里德曼在经济学学者中是无与伦比的，他为经济学做出了大量的原创性贡献，例如对于消费支出永恒收入理论的发展、对于货币经济学颠覆范式的研究；此外，他还在经济学历史与方法论方面撰写了多篇引人深思的原创性论文。"[8]

弗里德曼的职业成就是如此之高，以至于人们很难仅从一个维度来评价他的影响。尤其是他的著作涵盖了经济学和政治学的多个领域。此外，有一些主题在他的所有研究中贯穿始终。

首先，如上所述，弗里德曼的众多著作旨在批驳他所谓的"幼稚凯恩斯主义"——这是 20 世纪 70 年代以前的主流经济学观点。[9] 从这个意义上讲，弗里德曼是一位理论家*：他意在提出与凯恩斯不同的观点，并极力主张政府在经济中的作用应该受到限制。在此背景下，弗里德曼在经济政策方面的著作应当被视为一个更大使命的一部分，即使经济思维与政策转向自由市场原则。

意义

弗里德曼的著作数量庞大，且影响深远。1976 年，他被授予诺贝尔经济学奖，颁奖理由是他在消费分析领域、货币史和货币理论等方面取得了重大成就；此外，他还展示了经济稳定政策的复杂性。[10] 换言之，尽管弗里德曼在货币经济学方面的论著对其职业生涯非常重要，但这仍然只是其众多著作中的一部分而已。

在某些方面，《货币政策的作用》一文的重要性之所以得以延续，是与经济思想中货币主义理论的演进相联系的。20 世纪 60 年代，货币主义日益受到追捧。1968 年，弗里德曼论文的发表又为其提供了强大的推动力。但是，20 世纪七八十年代，该理论的热度开始下滑。经济学家班尼特·麦卡勒姆*认为，在这一时期，主张货币需求恒定的货币主义观点已经让位于认为"每个季度的货币需求都会发生显著且不可预期变化"的新观点。[11] 弗里德曼主张保持恒定货币增速的观点，在货币需求存在周期性波动的现实世界中，似乎并不可行。

货币主义的衰落也与现实事件有关。在 1979 年到 1982 年间，美联储试图进行"货币主义实验"，以降低 20 世纪 70 年代持续存在的高通胀率，并试图达到特定的货币供应增长月度目标。[12] 该实验收紧了货币供应，其效果是短期内抬高了利率，减少了商业活动，结果导致了"自 20 世纪 30 年代大萧条以来最严重的经济衰退"。[13] 今天，该实验被看作是抑制通货膨胀的一次必要尝试，但当时的观察家则将其视为"宏观经济的灾难"。[14]

尽管当前弗里德曼关于保持稳定货币政策的建议在一定程度上已经不再受到人们的青睐，但是他的思想的种子，尤其是他对于菲利普斯曲线的批评，至今仍具重要价值。

1. 米尔顿·弗里德曼:《消费功能理论》,新泽西州普林斯顿:普林斯顿大学出版社,1957 年。

2. "米尔顿·弗里德曼",经济学与自由图书馆,登录日期 2015 年 2 月 18 日,http://www.econlib.org/library/bios/Friedman.html。

3. 弗里德曼:《消费功能理论》,第 6 页。

4. 米尔顿·弗里德曼和安娜·施瓦茨:《美国货币史(1867—1960)》,新泽西州普林斯顿:普林斯顿大学出版社,1963 年。

5. 弗里德曼和施瓦茨:《美国货币史(1867—1960)》,第 301 页。

6. 米尔顿·弗里德曼:"从智利回国时致皮诺切特将军的信函与回信",最近登录日期 2015 年 2 月 18 日,http://www.naomiklein.org/files/resources/pdfs/friedman-pinochet-letters.pdf。

7. "米尔顿·弗里德曼:经济学家中的巨人",载《经济学人》,2006 年 11 月 23 日。

8. 伯南克:"米尔顿·弗里德曼九十华诞致辞",登录日期 2015 年 2 月 18 日,http://www.federalreserve.gov/boarddocs/Speeches/2002/20021108/default.htm。

9. "米尔顿·弗里德曼专访",公共广播服务,登录日期 2015 年 2 月 18 日,http://pbs.org/wgbh/commandingmheights/shared/minitext/int_miltonfriedman.html#7。

10. "米尔顿·弗里德曼:事实真相",Nobelprize.org,登录日期 2015 年 2 月 18 日,http://www.nobelprize.org/nobel_prizes/economic-sciences/laureates/1976/friedman-facts.html。

11. 班尼特·麦卡勒姆:"货币主义",经济学与自由图书馆,登录日期 2015 年 2 月 18 日 http://www.econlib.org/library/Enc/Monetarism.html。

12. 麦卡勒姆:"货币主义"。

13. 麦卡勒姆:"货币主义"。

14. 麦卡勒姆:"货币主义"。

第三部分：学术影响

9 最初反响

要点 ☖

- 对弗里德曼论文的批评性回应，主要来自凯恩斯主义经济学家。首当其冲的是，他们批驳了弗里德曼的以下观点，即政府将失业率降至弗里德曼所说的"自然"水平以下是毫无意义的。

- 20世纪70年代的"滞涨"*（指影响某些西方经济体的经济停滞和通货膨胀同时存在的状态）似乎支持了弗里德曼对于那种主张只要准备忍受高通胀就可以实现低失业率的观点的批驳，尽管该观点得到菲利普斯曲线的支持。

- 弗里德曼呼吁保持稳定的货币供应增长率，这一主张在今天看来是无效的。但是，弗里德曼所捍卫的货币主义理论仍然具有巨大的影响力，尤其是他认为，审慎的货币政策对于稳定经济是有效的。

批评

总体而言，对于弗里德曼观点的批评和争论大都集中于他的货币主义观点，而不是他在《货币政策的作用》一文中的具体论述。但是，仍有部分凯恩斯主义者直接对该论文提出了批评。

在批评弗里德曼的凯恩斯主义者当中，最引人注目的是詹姆士·托宾*。1971年，在对美国经济协会所做的演讲中，托宾对弗里德曼关于"自然"失业率的理解提出了质疑，而这一概念正是《货币政策的作用》一文分析的核心所在。弗里德曼认为，自然失业率源自经济的发展、劳动力的受教育程度等结构性特征，托宾则对这一概念的有效性提出了质疑。他认为，政府行为应当有能力将失业率降到任何所谓的"自然"失业率以下。"弗里德曼建议货币当局不要寻求改善自然失业率,但事实上,我们对于相关平衡状态的存在知之甚少,而这种状态允许所有缺陷与摩擦,又可解释为什么自然失业率是大于零的。"[1]

弗里德曼认为,政府对于一定范围内的失业率无能为力,这是因为任何经济体都存在一个雇工总量的上限。与此相反,托宾则认为,自然失业率可以通过适当的政府政策得到降低。[2]

弗里德曼也受到了来自货币主义者的批评。例如,除了针对弗里德曼的《货币政策的作用》一文之外,卡尔·布鲁纳*和艾伦·梅尔策*还针对其整体货币政策提出,弗里德曼的理论"对于实验性工作而言并不是一个特别有用的基础"。[3]他们认为,该理论太过模糊,并且批评其没有将"货币政策滞后现象(即货币政策调整与对经济产生影响之间的时间间隔)[4]的可变性"等实验成果吸收进来。

> "现在我是一名凯恩斯主义者。"
>
> —— 美国总统理查德·尼克松,1971

回应

在整个职业生涯中,弗里德曼对于菲利普斯曲线都坚定地表示了反对。作为一篇支持货币主义立场的公开演讲,弗里德曼将自己1976年诺贝尔奖获奖演说的大部分篇幅都用于阐述上述观点。他在此次演讲中指出,自己正在挑战大部分经济学家所持有的一个观点:"'自然'失业率或者加速主义假说或者受预期调节的菲利普斯曲线假设等各种称谓迄今已被经济学家广泛接受,尽管并非人人都

接受。"⁵

然后，他分三步提出了一个总结，用以说明人们对于菲利普斯曲线观点的变化过程。首先，他在简短的历史总结中论及了新西兰经济学家威廉·菲利普斯的观点，即通货膨胀和失业之间存在负相关关系。第二步是提出论点，该论点是由弗里德曼和经济学家埃德蒙·费尔普斯分别独立提出的。该论点认为，通货膨胀和失业之间的关联并不像菲利普斯所主张的那样简单。第三步，也是最后一步，就是提出弗里德曼所认为的一个上下颠倒的菲利普斯曲线："近些年来，更高的通货膨胀率往往伴随着更高而非更低的失业率，尤其是几年以后。"⁶这种滞涨情形——即整个20世纪70年代严重拖累美国和英国的经济停滞与高失业率相结合而同时伴随物价上涨的高通货膨胀的情形——被认为支持了弗里德曼对菲利普斯曲线的批评。

对于来自货币主义阵营的批评，弗里德曼则表示接受。他写道："总体上，我同意布鲁纳和梅尔策的批评意见，但他们并没有就我对于凯恩斯主义所作阐释的任何细节做出评论。之所以会出现分歧，仅仅是因为他们慷慨地高估了我的写作目标。"⁷作为友谊的表示，弗里德曼还在诺贝尔奖获奖演说中特地引用了布鲁纳和梅尔策的相关论述，但对托宾及其他凯恩斯主义者则未直接提及。

冲突与共识

弗里德曼提出，应当设立一个恒定的货币供应量增长规则，也就是说，货币供应量的增长应当与经济的长期增长率大致对应。这一主张现在已经不再受到政策制定者的青睐。但是，货币主义仍然为宏观经济和当前的政策制定做出了巨大而持久的贡献。美国经济学家班尼特·麦卡勒姆*写道："大多数研究型经济学家现在都接受或至少默认，货币政策比财政政策更有利于稳定经济"。[8]
进而，货币当局总体上接受了弗里德曼关于货币政策的作用与局
限的论断。

经济学家凯文·胡佛 * 的研究重点包含 20 世纪宏观经济学史。
他写道："20 世纪 70 年代为弗里德曼和费尔普斯的根本观点提供
了鲜明的支持。与最初的菲利普斯曲线相反，当平均通货膨胀率从
20 世纪 60 年代的 2.5% 左右上升到 70 年代的 7% 左右时，失业率
不仅没有下降，事实上还从大约 4% 上涨到了 6% 以上。"[9] 菲利普
斯曲线的上述反例，似乎挑战了托宾的观点，即政府对于市场的干
预能够使失业率降至接近于零。

此外，正如布赖恩·斯诺登和霍华德·R. 文所说，"也许货币
主义最重要、最持久的贡献在于使许多经济学家相信，积极的、放
任的财政和货币政策的潜力比货币主义者提出反对思想以前所想象
的更为有限。"[10]

换言之，最近几十年的经历对货币政策制定者产生了一种清醒
效果。那些在弗里德曼的论文发表之前相信政府应制定经济干预政
策的人发现，这些政策的作用并没有表面上看起来那样有效。在此
意义上，弗里德曼赢得了与凯恩斯主义的辩论。

---

1. 詹姆斯·托宾："通货膨胀与失业"，《美国经济评论》1972 年第 1 期，第 6 页。

2. 托宾："通货膨胀与失业"，第 15 页。

3. 卡尔·布鲁纳和艾伦·梅尔策："弗里德曼的货币理论"，《政治经济杂志》
1972 年第 5 期，第 837 页。

4. 布鲁纳和梅尔策:"弗里德曼的货币理论",第 849 页。

5. 米尔顿·弗里德曼:"通货膨胀与失业",1976 年 12 月 13 日诺贝尔纪念馆演讲,登录日期 2015 年 2 月 18 日,http://www.nobelprize.org/nobel_prizes/economic-sciences/laureates/1976/friedman-lecture.pdf。

6. 弗里德曼:"通货膨胀与失业"。

7. 米尔顿·弗里德曼:"批评家评论",《政治经济杂志》,第 80 卷 1972 年,第 907 页。

8. 班尼特·麦卡勒姆:"货币主义",经济学与自由图书馆,登录日期 2015 年 2 月 18 日,http://www.econlib.org/library/Enc/Monetarism.html。

9. 凯文·胡佛:"菲利普斯曲线",经济学与自由图书馆,登录日期 2015 年 2 月 18 日,http://www.econlib.org/libarary/Enc/PhillipsCurve.html。

10. 布赖恩·斯诺登和霍华德·R.文:《现代宏观经济学:起源、发展与现状》,切尔滕纳姆:爱德华·埃尔加出版社,2005 年,第 197 页。

10 后续争议

要点 ⚸━

- 弗里德曼的著作为宏观经济学的重要发展奠定了基础。这些发展中包括了"理性预期"*的研究方法。该方法假定，个人与公司会对通货膨胀等问题做出理性、准确的预测。

- 货币主义经济学派的发展，并非仅限于弗里德曼的著作。该学派仍在继续演化，但人们往往还是将其与弗里德曼关于保持稳定的货币供应增长的主张联系在一起，尽管这一主张现在几乎已经完全失去了人们的青睐。

- 在最近几十年中，一直存在货币主义与凯恩斯主义方式的融合，其追随者通常被称为"新凯恩斯主义者"。

应用与问题

弗里德曼的论文《货币政策的作用》和他的其他著作促成了宏观经济学数十年的发展。从该论文中产生的一个关键研究方法就是"理性预期"经济学，与之相关的经济学家包括罗伯特·卢卡斯和托马斯·萨金特。

卢卡斯的论文"预期和货币的中立性"（1972）以弗里德曼对于菲利普斯曲线的分析为研究起点建立了一种模型。在此模型中，"所有价格都恰好保持市场供需平衡，所有参与者都依据其目的和预期做出最优的表现。"——换言之，个人和公司都有能力在经济中做出完全理性的表现。[1]

这些假设与弗里德曼对于菲利普斯曲线的批评直接相关。弗里德曼表明，通货膨胀的上升之所以能够引起哪怕短期的就业提升，唯一原因就是：工人们并不会立刻注意到物价水平的上涨，以及他们的工资正在失去购买力。换言之，实际工资的下降使雇主有动力雇佣更多工人。但很快，工人们就会注意到通货膨胀，并且预期价格将会持续上涨。基于他们理性的预期，他们就会反过来要求加薪，以使他们的实际工资回到之前的水平。至此，通货膨胀就不再能够推高就业率。正如托马斯·萨金特所述，"理性预期破坏了政策制定者关于可以通过使公众产生虚假预期来操控经济的想法。"[2]

> "货币主义对于当今人们如何认识宏观经济，产生了深刻、普遍和细微的影响。"
>
> —— 布拉德福德·德龙：《货币主义的胜利？》

思想流派

自 20 世纪 60 年代中叶以来，与《货币政策的作用》一文相联系的货币主义学派经历了演变与发展。在许多方面，该学派一直与弗里德曼关于稳定增加货币供应的失败建议相联系。正如经济学家威廉·比特 * 在 2003 年所指出的，"弗里德曼关于保持货币总量（即货币储备）恒定增速的主张今天已经完全失去了人们的青睐，且在过去几十年中都是如此。"[3] 尽管大多数货币当局现在都会采纳弗里德曼的核心观点，即提供一个稳定的货币供应环境，但实际上没有任何一国的货币当局会支持采取固定的货币供应增长率。

换言之，弗里德曼关于货币政策的作用的观点是被政策制定者和经济学学科所接受的。但是，他关于货币政策应该如何制定与执行的诸多观点，却未被人们所接受。正如货币经济学家班尼特·麦卡勒姆指出的，"吸引大部分注意力的是弗里德曼关于保持货币供应恒定增速的规则，而不是货币主义中同等重要的其他基础方面，因此降低了人们对于货币主义的理解与欣赏。"[4]

麦卡勒姆继续指出，货币主义今天的核心特征都源自弗里德曼对于菲利普斯曲线的批评。货币主义对于凯恩斯主义批评的主要内容至今仍然被人们认为是正确的，主要包括：实际变量和名义变量之间的区分，以及对于在通货膨胀和失业之间存在长期替代关系的观点的否定。[5]

当代研究

颇具讽刺意味的是，在今天的经济学辩论当中，大多数具有货币主义传统的专家都很可能自认为是"新凯恩斯主义者"。这是因为在 20 世纪 80 年代和 90 年代，货币主义与凯恩斯主义的观点发生了融合。根据最受瞩目的新凯恩斯主义专家之一——格里高利·曼昆 * 的观点，"新凯恩斯主义者"指的是那些用修正的凯恩斯主义原则回应新古典货币主义学派的人。[6]

常与政治左翼相关联的经济学家布拉德福德·德龙 * 认为，新凯恩斯主义理论体系包含五个组成部分，其中一些内容直接来自弗里德曼的货币主义理论。

第一，新凯恩斯主义者相信，经济中的阻力——如繁琐的规则、买家和卖家的信息缺乏以及其他潜在障碍——是引起经济波动（涨落）即所谓商业周期的首要原因。

第二，他们相信，在稳定经济方面，货币政策比财政政策更强大、更有用。

第三，商业周期最适宜被分析为对于"可持续的长期趋势的背离"。

第四，实施宏观经济政策的最佳方式是应用规则，而不是对每个孤立的事件进行单独的分析。

第五，任何实现经济稳定的方式都必须承认"稳定政策的局限性"。[7]

上述观点与弗里德曼论述的相似性是显而易见的。弗里德曼对于菲利普斯曲线的挑战就提醒了人们经济稳定政策的局限性。而且，弗里德曼一直主张货币政策比财政政策更为重要。此外，遵循总体政策规则的方式也可视为与弗里德曼关于保持货币供应稳定增长的建议相类似。正如德龙所指出的，"以上所列的新凯恩斯主义的五个组成部分，在其发展中大体都可以找到 20 世纪货币主义传统的影子，并且都与米尔顿·弗里德曼的名字相关联。"[8]

1. 罗伯特·卢卡斯："预期和货币的中立性"，《经济理论杂志》，1972 年第 4 期，第 103 页。

2. 托马斯·萨金特："理性预期"，最近登录日期 2015 年 2 月 18 日，http://www.econlib.org/library/Enc/RationalExpectations.html。

3. 布赖恩·斯诺登和霍华德·R. 文：《现代宏观经济学：起源、发展与现状》，切尔滕纳姆：爱德华·埃尔加出版社，2005 年，第 196 页。

4. 班尼特·麦卡勒姆："货币主义"，经济学与自由图书馆，登录日期 2015 年 2 月 18 日，http://www.econlib.org/library/Enc/Monetarism.html。

5. 麦卡勒姆："货币主义"。

6. 格瑞格里·曼昆："新凯恩斯主义经济学"，经济学与自由图书馆，登录日期 2015 年 2 月 18 日，http://www.econlib.org/library/Enc/NewKeynesianEconomics.html。

7. 布拉德福德·德龙："凯恩斯主义的胜利？"，《经济视角杂志》，2000 年第 1 期，第 83—84 页。

8. 德龙："凯恩斯主义的胜利？"。

11 当代印迹

要点 ⚿━

- 弗里德曼的论文仍然具有重要意义，其中关于货币当局应当采取和不应当采取的货币政策的诸多建议已被广为接受。

- 作为一名顶尖的经济学家、货币主义的开创者和自由市场的倡导者，弗里德曼在公共领域具有广泛影响力。

- 主张加大政府对经济干预者和主张减少政府对经济干预者之间的争论总体上仍然呈现出两极化趋势。

地位

弗里德曼的论文《货币政策的作用》至今仍然是学术争论的一个重要部分。总体而言，论文关于成功的货币当局所应扮演的"恰当"角色的许多观点，已经被人们所接受。但是关于如何执行货币政策的问题，本身仍然是一个非常重要并且在不断发展的学术和政策争论的问题。该问题关系到整个经济学学科。

在论文中，弗里德曼将经济想象为一系列相互关联的机械装置，并强调，"当货币政策发生损坏时，就相当于把一只活动扳手扔到正在运转的所有其他机器当中去。"[1] 结果在处理政府开支和国际贸易等问题时，几乎所有的经济学家在某个阶段都需要解释货币和货币政策的作用问题。

在论文《再论货币政策的作用》中，经济学家约翰·柯克伦强调了弗里德曼的观点在当代争论中的重要性。例如，他问道："我们当今的政策实验当中还有多少像 1968 年菲利普斯曲线那样的错误？"[2]

更准确地说，柯克伦指出：当前旨在刺激经济的"量化宽松"的货币政策——即中央银行从商业银行买入金融资产的政策——也许太过于乐观。就美国最近的情形而言，美联储的量化宽松政策"将货币储备从500亿美元暴增至3万亿美元，尽管如此，国内生产总值仍然有待真正实现从衰退中复苏。因此你必须提出疑问，这种做法有效吗？是时候开始像弗里德曼一样思考并评估这些政策了。与此同时，我们需要寻求一个更加清晰、简洁的理论基础。"

> "（它）是战后最具决定意义的经济学成就之一。"
> —— 保罗·克鲁格曼评弗里德曼对于"滞涨"——20世纪70年代影响美、英经济的失业与通货膨胀同时增加的情况——的预测

互动

弗里德曼的诸多思想已经完全被融入了当代经济学理论，那些没有被融入的思想现在已经失去了人们的青睐。例如，现在学术界很少有兴趣再去重新审视弗里德曼关于恒定货币供应的假设。[3]

在此前提下，关于弗里德曼影响的许多批评性争论主要是围绕其政治立场以及其货币政策在国际上的应用情况。弗里德曼的许多批评者都是政治上的左翼人士，因此他们对其在美国和世界其他地方促进自由市场的行为提出质疑。产生这种质疑的部分原因在于弗里德曼身份复杂。保罗·克鲁格曼写道："弗里德曼在生活中有三种不同的角色——'经济学家的引路人'、货币主义的政策先锋，以及作为自由市场信条重要传播者的'理论家弗里德曼'"。[4]这三种角色中的最后一种正是他受到批评的主要原因。尽管如此，弗里德曼当然也因为他对于货币主义的宣传而受到批评。

克鲁格曼也考察了弗里德曼与美国政治右翼之间的不平衡关系。他写道："结果表明，相对于美国现代政治右翼而言，弗里德曼过于注重细节和现实主义，而美国政治右翼则通常不注重细节，并且拒绝现实。"[5] 尽管克鲁格曼在此方面对弗里德曼表达了有限的支持，但他也刻意保持了与弗里德曼之间的距离。他写道："我认为，日本以及整个西方世界过去 15 年的先后经历都表明，在货币政策是否有能力独立应对经济萧条的问题上，凯恩斯是对的，弗里德曼是错的。事实上，我们需要一个更加积极有为的政府，而弗里德曼却不愿承认这一点。"[6]

上述评论反映了弗里德曼当前在政治和经济辩论中的地位。对于有些人而言，弗里德曼被视作一个右翼的混蛋；而对于其他人而言，他则是一个自由主义的英雄。但是，他的许多思想表现了务实的本质，这为人们对他做出更为细致的评价提供了机会。

持续争议

弗里德曼的许多挑战者认为，尽管弗里德曼的出发点是好的，但是他的建议却并不成功。弗里德曼逝世后，英国《卫报》的教育编辑理查德·亚当斯在一篇名为《弗里德曼：失败案例研究》的文章中提出，尽管弗里德曼是位伟大的经济学家，但他的大部分思想，包括货币主义的核心观点在内，在政治和经济方面都是失败的。[7] 亚当斯指出，弗里德曼关于央行应为货币供应量的增长设立固定规则的建议，在 20 世纪七八十年代经过试验被证明并不成功并遭到抛弃。"今天，没有哪个主要国家的央行会直接将货币供应数据作为货币政策的设定目标。相反，他们现在更为务实。"[8]

也有其他批评者对弗里德曼提出了道德层面的质疑，其中以作家娜奥米·克莱因最为知名。克莱因提到，20 世纪 70 年代中叶，智利发生了右翼军事政变，弗里德曼曾在智利经济全面改革中担任顾问。这一改革被克莱因称作"有史以来最为极端的资本主义的改造。"克莱因写道："'这场像步枪速射一样的经济转变'实际上是一次不必要的'冲击'"。此外，克莱因表示，这场经济变革的动机是支持自由企业，而非想要促进社会公共利益。[9]克莱因的批评准确反映了弗里德曼的观点。弗里德曼是自由市场思想的公共代言人，也是20世纪七八十年代席卷发展中国家的公共机构私有化运动的幕后策划者。克莱因认为，弗里德曼是"自由放任资本主义思想的精神领袖"，正是他"为当代高度动态的全球经济书写了规则手册。"

1. 米尔顿·弗里德曼："货币政策的作用"，《美国经济评论》第58卷，1968年3月1日第1期，第12页。

2. 约翰·柯克伦："再论货币政策的作用"，登录日期2015年2月18日，http://bfi.uchicago.edu/feature-story/role-monetary-policy-revisited。

3. 柯克伦："再论货币政策的作用"。

4. 保罗·克鲁格曼："米尔顿·弗里德曼是谁？"，登录日期2015年2月18日，http://www.nybooks.com/articles/archives/2007/feb/15/who-was-milton-friedman/。

5. 保罗·克鲁格曼："米尔顿·弗里德曼：没落之神"，登录日期2015年2月18日，http://www.nytimes.com/2013/08/12/opinion/krugman-milton-friedman-unperson.html?smid=tw-share&_r=0。

6. 克鲁格曼："米尔顿·弗里德曼：没落之神"。

7. 理查德·亚当斯："弗里德曼：失败案例研究"，《卫报》，登录日期2015年2月18日，http://www.theguardian.com/commentisfree/2006/nov/16/post650。

8. 亚当斯："弗里德曼：失败案例研究"。

9. 娜奥米·克莱因：《休克学说》，登陆日期2015年2月18日，http://www.naomiklein.org/shock-doctrine/excerpt。

12 未来展望

要点 🗝

- 该论文仍然是讨论货币政策对于更大范围内宏观经济稳定所起作用的入门文献。

- 央行可用的政策工具已经得到扩展。与此同时，在介入更大范围的经济微调方面，央行受到的诱惑也随之增加。但是，一个核心问题仍然存在，即短期收益是否会被潜在的长期后果所抵消？

- 弗里德曼的论文清楚地揭示了过于积极的货币政策的危险，这对于 20 世纪抵制政府过度干预经济起到了关键作用。

潜力

2008 年至 2010 年的金融危机凸显了市场经济持续的不稳定性。这场危机也表明，货币政策的制定者正不断试图适应经济运行的新信息和新任务。很难预测 21 世纪的货币政策究竟会怎样演化，但是有两点似乎是合理而清晰的。首先，弗里德曼已经永久性改变了如何看待货币当局在提供稳定的经济基础方面的作用的问题。其二，弗里德曼关于采取稳定的货币供应增长率的建议不太可能再次被尝试，因为显然有必要使用货币政策来消除经济波动（必要时调整货币供应）。

正如经济学家约翰·柯克伦所说的那样，弗里德曼的论文未来很有可能将继续保持其重要性，可以提醒人们注意经济干预的局限性。随着经济管理变得日益复杂，这些教训只会变得更为重要。

例如，可以试想一下货币政策在政府遇到巨大债务时所能发挥的作用："每年美国都会收入 2.5 万亿美元，支出 3.5 万亿美元，我们的现有债务高达 16 万亿美元，未来还将欠下无数美元。"柯克伦表示，"如果联邦政府决定收紧货币政策，并将利率设定为 5%，那么，16 万亿美元的债务每年将会增加 8,000 亿美元的新赤字。"经济条件的变化为政策制定者提出了新的挑战，《货币政策的作用》一文将继续充当下列经验的参考，即："货币政策可以伤害经济"，货币政策制定者必须谨慎行事。[1]

> "货币政策本身无法实现一组更广泛、更平衡的经济政策所能达成的目标，尤其是它无法消除国家所面临的财政和金融风险，它当然也不能对经济成果进行微调。"
>
> —— 本杰明·伯南克，美联储主席

未来方向

有位经济学家处理货币政策的方式与弗里德曼几乎一致，他就是拉格拉姆·拉詹*，现任印度储备银行（即印度央行）行长。与弗里德曼一样，拉詹观点的出发点是他对自由市场的强烈信任以及对财政政策（即通过政府开支来刺激经济）的怀疑。例如，为了应对 2008 年至 2010 年的金融危机，拉詹认为，应当推动根本性的经济变革，如为新的全球经济的不同岗位培养更多训练有素的人才，使税务结构更加有利于创业等，而不是采取政府经济刺激项目：

"当今的经济麻烦，不仅源于需求的不足，而且同样源于商业和经济增长环境的不利。在 2008 年金融危机前的几十年中，发达经济体一直在丧失通过制造有用商品来实现增长的能力。"[2]

在这场当代版辩论中，一方是支持财政刺激政策的凯恩斯主义者，另一方是主张改革经济基本面的自由市场的支持者，拉詹所扮演的正是弗里德曼的角色。

另一位与弗里德曼表现出相近方式的经济学家是纳兰尼娅·柯切拉科塔＊，现任明尼阿波利斯联邦储备银行总裁，尽管弗里德曼和柯切拉科塔也许无法在若干原则上达成共识。柯切拉科塔采取的一项行动也许会让人们想起弗里德曼对于以逐步调整价格为目标的货币政策的支持。在此项行动中，柯切拉科塔认为，美联储必须更加清楚地表明其对达到通胀目标的预期。例如，在近期的一次讲话中，柯切拉科塔就提出，想要"价格稳定"，就需清晰阐述联邦政府实现通胀目标的时间表。[3]

小结

《货币政策的作用》一文至今仍是一个包含非凡原创力和深刻洞察力的杰作，提供了预测未来发展的力量。该文成功挑战并推翻了当时尚被广泛接受的凯恩斯主义的理论基础，并且改变了随后几十年中货币政策的走向，使得政策制定者得以从先前的错误中吸取教训，避免经济问题与经济危机恶化。鉴于此，该文对于政策制定者和经济学学生仍将具有重要意义。

正是因为弗里德曼对于凯恩斯主义经济学的批判性分析力度较大，才使得这篇论文区别于其他的学术著作。在短短 17 页的论述当中，弗里德曼有力地挑战了此前几十年中制定政策的理论基础，奠定了货币主义学派的基础，并永久性改变了当时人们普遍接受的诸多假设。

该文的读者不仅可以深入了解美国货币政策的演变历史，而且还可以学习到经济分析的杰出范例。尽管许多经济学论文技术性都很强，并且有些抽象，但《货币政策的作用》一文将会帮助人们思考一些金融报道中的事件，以便更好地理解周围的世界。此外，由于弗里德曼是 20 世纪最重要的经济学家之一，阅读该论文将使学生有机会接触到围绕经济学所进行的公开辩论中的一些最基本的问题，比如，政府对于经济政策的重要性究竟如何？究竟怎样的政策才能切实有效？

---

1. 约翰·柯克伦："再论货币政策的作用"，登录日期 2015 年 2 月 18 日，http://bfi. uchicago.edu/feature-story/role-monetary-policy-revisited。

2. 拉格拉姆·拉詹："金融危机的真正教训"，《外交》，登录日期 2015 年 2 月 18 日，http://www.foreignaffairs.com/articles/134863/raghuram-g-rajan/the-true-lessons-of-the-recession。

3. 纳兰尼娅·柯切拉科塔："价格稳定的含义辨析"，登录日期 2015 年 2 月 18 日，https://www.minneapolisfed.org/publications/the-region/clarifying-the-meaning-of-price-stability。

术语表

1. **总需求**：经济体系中在某个特定时间对于商品和服务的需求总量。

2. **商业周期**：一个经济学概念，指在数年内经济因繁荣（增长）和萧条（收缩）交替发生而呈现的起伏波动。经济的扩张与收缩一般围绕经济的长期增长趋势发生周期变化。

3. **资本主义**：一种由私人控制工业与贸易的经济制度。在资本主义制度下，私人对自己的商品与服务拥有所有权，同时，市场是贸易开展的场所。

4. **芝加哥（经济）学派**：来自芝加哥大学的一群经济学家，主要特征是：信仰新古典主义经济学，尤其推崇价格理论，并普遍相信市场的力量。

5. **古典主义经济学传统**：经济学的第一个现代学派，代表人物有：亚当·斯密、大卫·李嘉图、托马斯·马尔萨斯、约翰·斯图亚特·穆勒。该学派活跃于18世纪晚期至19世纪中晚期。古典主义经济学家普遍相信市场能够自我调节。

6. **消费者选择**：可供普通大众消费者购买的各类产品与服务。

7. **消费**：经济中购买行为的总称。

8. **通货紧缩**：商品供应量远大于货币供应量时出现的现象，它导致商品价格下跌。

9. **萧条**：经济持续下行。在美国，尤指国内生产总值下跌超过10%，或经济持续衰退超过两年以上。

10. **劳动分工**：合作生产者因专业化分工而承担生产过程中的某项具体任务。

11. **经济增长**：在一定时期内，经济体所产生的商品和服务总量的增加。

12. **经济指标**：经济的可测量特征，如通货膨胀或失业等的统计数据。

13. **汇率**：货币间的兑换比率。

14. **美联储（美国联邦储备系统）**：美国中央银行系统，负责管理美国货币和金融政策。

15. **2008年至2010年金融危机**：源自美国的一场经济危机，波及欧洲大部分区域与其他地区，被认为是20世纪30年代以来最严重的金融危机。

16. **财政政策**：利用政府开支影响经济的政策，包含社会项目开支、税收以及公路、桥梁等公共基础设施项目开支等。

17. **财政刺激**：通过增加消费或降低税收以增加政府开支的政策，目标通常是降低失业及促进经济增长。

18. **自由市场**：市场中商品和服务的交易受价格体系调节的市场系统。自由市场通常区别于中央计划经济。

19. **自由贸易**：对国家间商品和服务交易不予限制的政策。与自由贸易相对的是通过征收关税对商品和服务的进出口实施限制。

20. **大萧条**：二十世纪持续时间最长、程度最严重的经济萧条，始自1929年底的美国股市崩溃，美国失业率飙升至25%，而其他国家失业率则超过30%。许多国家直至二战结束才开始漫长的复苏。

21. **国内生产总值与国民生产总值**：国内生产总值（GDP）是最重要的经济指标之一，反映特定时间内一国境内所有商品与服务的市场价值总和。国民生产总值（GNP）则指特定时间内一国国民生产的所有商品与服务的市场价值总和，与生产地无关。例如，位于肯尼亚的美资工厂的产值将计入美国GNP，但不计入美国GDP。

22. **增长率**：特定时间周期内的经济增长幅度。

23. **理论家**：坚定不移地信奉特定理论或学说并有稳固地位者。

24. **通货膨胀**：货币供应量远大于商品供应量时出现的现象，导致商品价格上涨。

25. **利率**：借贷的成本。美国联邦储备银行通过调节联邦基金利率来调控利率。

26. **犹太人**：指犹太教信徒。犹太教于 3500 多年前在中东创立。如今，犹太人主要生活在以色列和美国，另有少量犹太人口分布在世界上其他国家。

27. **凯恩斯主义**：一种经济学流派，提出经济性市场无法自我修正，主张积极的政府政策有助于稳定经济，这些政策包括政府支出（财政政策）以及控制货币供应量（货币政策）。

28. **自由放任**：一个经济学概念，指政府不干预经济并放任市场自由波动的状态。

29. **左翼**：政治体制或政党中传统上偏向社会主义或改革的派别。

30. **意志自由论（自由主义）**：一种政治学流派，主张个人行为应享有近乎绝对自由，政府干预作用应降至最低。

31. **宏观经济学**：研究宏观经济表现的经济学分支。

32. **重商主义**：16 至 18 世纪欧洲所奉行的一种经济体制，禁止国家间自由贸易，鼓励政府通过削弱竞争对手以积累财富。亚当·斯密在其《国富论》中对重商主义进行了批判，并论述了自由贸易的好处。

33. **微观经济学**：研究个人及公司层面决策过程的经济学分支。

34. **货币主义**：一种经济学观点，主张调整货币供应量虽可在短期内对失业等经济指标产生显著影响，但长期则不然。强调实际价格与名义价格的区分，并认为货币政策应该遵循规则，以便创造稳定的经济预期。

35. **货币经济学**：研究货币的经济功能的经济学分支，其核心问题是各类货币总量之间的关系，如货币供应量与就业等经济变量之间的关系。

36. **货币政策**：控制某一经济区域内货币供应量的机制，"扩张性"货币政策增加货币供应量，"收缩性"货币政策减少货币供应量。货币当局的货币政策目标是保持物价稳定及维持低失业率。货币政策区别于财政政策，后者涉及税收、政府开支及借贷。

37. **货币供应**：经济体在特定时间内的货币资产总量。

38. **新凯恩斯主义**：一个经济学流派，主张综合运用理性预期、古典经济学和凯恩斯主义经济理论。

39. **诺贝尔经济学奖**：又称"瑞典国家银行奖"，每年一次的崇高殊荣，颁发给为经济学做出重大贡献的经济学家。

40. **名义价值**：经济学中，名义价值的标称与特定历史时期有关，而实际价值则反映价格及其他随时间而发生的变化。例如，1930年，一辆汽车的名义价格远低于现在的名义价格，但是，转换成购买力的实际价格却很可能高于现在。

41. **持久收入假说**：一种经济学观点，即任何特定时段内的消费（即对商品与服务的支出），不仅与个人当前收入有关，还与其可预期的未来收入相关。

42. **菲利普斯曲线**：衡量通货膨胀率（通胀率）与失业率关系的曲线。根据该曲线，低失业率与高通胀率相关，显示失业率和通胀率二者之间存在此消彼长的关系。

43. **价格水平**：经济体内整体价格水平的指数或数值。价格水平的变动取决于通货膨胀率。

44. **价格理论**：一种经济学理论，其理论基础是商品或服务的价格取决于其供求关系。

45. **购买力**：使用特定单位数量的货币所能购买的商品与服务的数量。

46. **量化宽松**：一项货币政策，表现为中央银行从商业银行购入金融资产，拉高金融资产价格，并增加基础货币供给。

47. **理性预期**：一种经济学理论，其基础假设是经济主体对未来做出准确理性的预测。

48. **实际价值**：经济学中，实际价值是经过调整的，以反映随时间而发生的价格和其他变化。而名义价值的标称与特定历史时期有关，例如，1930 年，一辆汽车的名义价格远低于现在的名义价格，但是，按购买力转换的实际价格却很可能高于现在。

49. **稀缺性**：由有限资源与无限需求所引发的经济学问题。由于无限资源不具有内在经济价值，故经济学家只研究稀缺资源。

50. **滞涨**：经济学术语，指高通货膨胀与高失业率同时发生的情形。

51. **股票市场**：金融股票及债券的交易场所。

52. **失业**：找工作的人找不到工作的状态。

53. **第二次世界大战**：1939 年至 1945 年以欧洲和太平洋地区为中心的一场世界战争。战争的双方是同盟国（美国、英国、苏联、中国等）与轴心国（德国、意大利、日本等）。

人名表

1. 本·伯南克（1953年生），美国经济学家，前美国联邦储备委员会主席，曾为全球最有影响力的货币政策制定者。

2. 卡尔·布鲁纳（1916—1989），瑞士经济学家，货币主义经济学派的关键成员之一，常常抨击美国联邦储备系统。

3. 威廉·比特（1949年生），美裔英国经济学家，以货币经济学著作而闻名。

4. 约翰·柯克伦（1957年生），美国经济学家，以联结金融与宏观经济学的著作而闻名。

5. 布拉德福德·德龙（1960年生），美国经济学家，为货币主义经济学及经济学史做出了贡献，最广为人知的身份可能是知名博主。

6. 欧文·费舍尔（1867—1947），美国经济学家，一般被认为是新古典主义经济学家。该学派有三条核心假设：人有基于价值的理性且可觉察的偏好；人追求最大效用，而企业追求最大利润；人的行为以掌握充分且相关的信息为前提。他被认为是"货币主义"宏观经济学派的创始人。

7. 戈特弗里德·哈伯勒（1900—1995），奥地利裔美国经济学家，最为知名的思想可能是比较优势与贸易。

8. 凯文·胡佛（1955年生），美国经济学家，研究经济学哲学与方法论，尤其关注因果分析。

9. 哈里·约翰逊（1923—1977），加拿大经济学家，主要研究国际贸易与国际金融，是货币主义经济学派的成员。

10. 约翰·梅纳德·凯恩斯（1883—1946），英国经济学家，其对于宏观经济学理论的贡献在经济政策制定中影响力巨大。他反对同时代的主流观点，提出经济放缓是由总需求不足引起的，此时政府应当介入，增加经济开支以提振需求。

11. **娜奥米·克莱因**（1970 年生），加拿大作家，最知名的作品包括《休克学说》、《没有标识》，对全球资本主义的基础提出质疑。

12. **纳兰尼娅·柯切拉科塔**（1963 年生），美国经济学家，明尼阿波利斯联邦储备银行行长。2008—2010 金融危机期间因在货币政策上改变观点而出名。

13. **保罗·克鲁格曼**（1953 年生），美国经济学家，2008 年因国际贸易研究获得诺贝尔奖。另一个享有广泛知名度的身份是《纽约时报》的政经评论员。

14. **罗伯特·卢卡斯**（1937 年生），美国经济学家，以提出理性预期经济学方法而著称，是芝加哥经济学派的重要成员。

15. **埃里克·伦德伯格**（1907—1987），瑞典经济学家，1975 年至 1979 年担任诺贝尔经济学奖评选委员会主席。

16. **格里高利·曼昆**（1958 年生），美国宏观经济学家，著有在美国颇为流行的大学本科经济学教材《经济学原理》。作为政府公务员，2003 年至 2005 年在小布什总统政府中担任美国经济顾问理事会主席。

17. **卡尔·马克思**（1818—1883），德国哲学家，其著作《资本论》和《共产党宣言》是共产主义的理论基础。

18. **班尼特·麦卡勒姆**（1935 年生），美国经济学家，将统计方法引入货币主义经济学研究。

19. **小威廉·麦克切斯尼·马丁**（1906—1998），美国政治家，1951 年至 1970 年担任美国联邦储备委员会主席，曾为五位美国总统效力。

20. **艾伦·梅尔泽**（1928 年生），美国经济学家，奉行货币主义传统，2012 年至 2014 年任佩勒林山学会主席，该学会致力于推进政治和经济自由。

21. **埃德蒙·费尔普斯**（1933 年生），美国经济学家，以对经济增长根源、储蓄率、价格—工资相互作用等研究而著称，在此基础上提出了自然失业率理论。2006 年获得诺贝尔经济学奖。

22. 威廉·菲利普斯（1914—1975），新西兰经济学家，最著名的经济学贡献是发现了通货膨胀与失业之间的负相关关系，以菲利普斯曲线而著称。

23. 奥古斯托·皮诺切特（1915—2006），1974年发动军事政变推翻民选总统后，担任智利第30任总统，直至1990年。任内以经济私有化而著称。

24. 拉格拉姆·拉詹（1963年生），印度经济学家，印度储备银行行长，主要研究领域包括金融、公司财务、经济发展等。

25. 罗纳德·里根（1911—2004），美国第40任总统，以"里根经济学"著称，主要政策包括减税、控制货币供应、给经济松绑以促进增长。

26. 莱昂内尔·罗宾斯（1898—1984），英国经济学家，以与约翰·梅纳德·凯恩斯展开持久论战而著称，此外还给"经济学"下了一个流行的定义。

27. 阿道夫·萨巴斯（1866—1952），美国政治家，从1907年至去世一直代表伊利诺伊州担任国会众议员。

28. 保罗·萨缪尔森（1915—2009），美国经济学家，为宏观经济学做出了重要贡献，有人认为他是"现代经济学之父"。

29. 托马斯·萨金特（1943年生），美国经济学家，开发统计技术并用以研究理性预期假设。

30. 安娜·施瓦茨（1915—2012），美国经济学家，最为知名的著作是其与米尔顿·弗里德曼合著的《美国货币史（1867—1960）》，从根本上改变了人们对于大萧条起因和货币经济学的理解。

31. 罗伯特·斯基德尔斯基（1939年生），英国经济历史学家，最为知名的著作可能是他为约翰·梅纳德·凯恩斯写的三卷本传记。

32. 亚当·斯密（1723—1790），苏格兰哲学家与政治经济学家，最有名的著作包括《道德情感理论》（1759）、《国富论》（1776），后者被公认为第一部现代经济学著作。

33. **罗伯特·索洛**（1924 年生），美国经济学家，帮助建立了经济增长理论，尤其是索洛增长模型。

34. **乔治·斯蒂格勒**（1911—1991），芝加哥大学经济学家，最为知名的研究是"规制俘虏理论"，即利益团体利用政府规制力量为自身利益服务。

35. **玛格丽特·撒切尔**（1925—2013），英国政治家，1979 年至 1990 年担任英国首相，是英国第一位女首相。其主要政策旨在限制政府干涉经济并刺激自由企业。

36. **詹姆斯·托宾**（1918—2002），美国经济学家，对金融进行了开拓性研究，也研究了货币和财政政策的应用，是凯恩斯主义流派主要成员。

37. **克努特·维克塞尔**（1851—1926），瑞典经济学家，最有影响的贡献是利息理论，其著作被认为是宏观经济学的基础。

WAYS IN TO THE TEXT

- Milton Friedman was a Nobel Prize*-winning American economist and one of the twentieth century's most influential economic thinkers. He made key contributions to consumer theory (the analysis of sales and purchases), monetary economics* (the understanding of what happens when a government controls the amount of money available in an economy), and economic methodology (the methods used to study economics).

- Friedman's essay "The Role of Monetary Policy" outlines the problems with the monetary policy widely followed in the 1950s and 1960s and highlights the dangers of governments using the money supply* and interest rates* to try to adjust economic growth* and unemployment.*

- The essay was one of the most important economic policymaking texts of the twentieth century and a foundational piece in the school of monetarism*—the viewpoint that there can be advantages to adjusting the amount of money in circulation in an economy.

Who Was Milton Friedman?

Milton Friedman (1912–2006), the author of "The Role of Monetary Policy," was one of the most influential economists of all time. During his long and productive academic career, he made major contributions to the fields of macroeconomics* (the understanding of what an economy is and how it functions on the large scale), consumption theory* (roughly, the theory of sales and purchases), the methodology of economics (the methods used to study economics), and economic history.

Beyond his academic work, Friedman was known as an avid supporter of free-market* economics and individual liberty. His public lectures and publications, particularly the books *Capitalism and Freedom* (1962) and *Free to Choose* (1980), presented his libertarian* beliefs—freedom for the individual and minimal government interference—to a large audience and helped popularize free-market thinking.

Friedman was born in 1912 in New York City in the United States to first-generation Jewish* immigrants from Eastern Europe. Although his parents were not rich, they instilled in him a sense of ambition and self-reliance. Friedman graduated from Rutgers University in the state of New Jersey in 1932, during the catastrophic economic collapse known as the Great Depression.* The effects of this recession, both economic and intellectual, would inform his entire career. Of this time, Friedman says: "Though 1932–33, my first year at Chicago, was, financially, my most difficult year, intellectually, it opened new worlds ...."[1]

After obtaining a Master's in Economics from the University of Chicago in 1933, Friedman completed his PhD in Economics at Columbia University in 1946. That year, he began teaching full-time at the University of Chicago.

Friedman's relationship with the University of Chicago is a notable part of the impact he had. He was a key member of the "Chicago school of economics"*—a group of scholars associated with the university who shared a common belief that governments should not intervene in an economy, and a common interest in price theory.* According to price theory, the value of a thing depends on the relationship between supply (how easy that thing is to obtain) and demand (how much that thing is wanted).

The Chicago school is also associated with the monetarist approach to macroeconomic policy—that is, economic policy for the economy as a whole. Friedman lays out many parts of this policy in "The Role of Monetary Policy."

Friedman's association with the Chicago school has both supported and hurt his reputation. On the one hand, as one of the school's leading voices, it is likely that he was able to reach a larger audience than he would have through his academic work alone. On the other hand, the school, along with its most vocal promoters, has been a frequent target of left-wing* critics such as the Canadian author and activist Naomi Klein,* who oppose the free-market ideology it supports.[2]

What Does "The Role of Monetary Policy" Say?

Published in 1968, "The Role of Monetary Policy" was a challenge to the position that monetary policy (that is, a government's decision to increase or limit the amount of money available in an economy) is an effective tool for achieving long-term targets for inflation* and unemployment. That position was promoted by the so-called Keynesian* economists, who agreed with the English economist John Maynard Keynes* (1883–1846) that government spending on things such as public works benefitted the economy as a whole by stimulating employment, demand, and economic growth. This was the most widely accepted approach to economics when Friedman's book first appeared.

Friedman had a specific target in mind: the Phillips Curve,* a theory presented by William Phillips,* an economist from New Zealand, that suggests a negative relationship between inflation and unemployment. The theory states, in other words, that when inflation increases, unemployment will fall, and vice versa.

The promise of the Phillips Curve, which was fully worked out by the American economists Paul Samuelson* and Robert Solow* in 1960, is that monetary policy could be used as an instrument to achieve desired economic outcomes. If, for example, the monetary authority (generally a country's central bank) wanted to decrease unemployment, it could do so by increasing the money supply, which would drive up inflation as more money chases after the same amount of goods. So inflation and unemployment are trade-offs.

Friedman did not entirely agree, seeing this view of monetary policy as far too optimistic. It failed to take into account, he believed, that if people expect prices or wages to change, they change their behavior, and it ignored the crucial difference between real values* and nominal values.* While *nominal* values are simply the stated value of a good or a service, *real* values take into account price changes over time. For example: suppose your nominal wage is ten dollars per hour. If after every year the nominal wage stays the same but the cost of living goes up, then your real wage will actually fall over time. Friedman applies this idea to the Phillips Curve.

Suppose the monetary authority wants to decrease unemployment. According to the Phillips Curve, it can do so by increasing inflation. Due to the fact that the selling prices of goods tend to increase faster than nominal wages (the actual amount on workers' paychecks), this will drive down real wages. However, after a while this will cause employees to demand higher wages or drop out of the labor force. Unemployment then rises to its previous level. Friedman calls that rate the "natural rate of unemployment," and assumes it is more or less stable.[3]

He concludes this analysis by saying: "[The monetary authority] cannot use its control over nominal quantities to peg a real quantity—the real rate of interest, the rate of unemployment, the level of real national income, the real quantity of money, the rate of growth of the real national income, or the rate of growth of the real quantity of money."[4] In other words, Friedman shows that while the Phillips Curve may hold in the short run, in the long run it will reverse, and thus policymakers are unwise to follow a policy based on it.

While much of Friedman's paper is concerned with the limitations of monetary policy, he concludes with suggestions for what policymakers can and should do. Most importantly, he suggests the goal of monetary policy should be to provide a steady money base for the economy in order to manage expectations and avoid unexpected shocks. Specifically, this means "adopting publicly the policy of achieving a steady rate of growth in a specified monetary total."[5]

In other words, Friedman is not so much concerned with the actual level of the economy's money supply (the amount of money available). His concern is that the money supply should increase at a constant rate and that its increase is transparent.[6]

This rule of a steady increase of the money supply was central to monetary policy for more than a decade following the publication of Friedman's paper.

Why Does "The Role of Monetary Policy" Matter?

Although it is only 17 pages long, "The Role of Monetary Policy" is a key text in economics. The paper paved the way for the widespread adoption of the monetarist approach to macroeconomics and the impact of this is felt to this day. But it also predicted economic problems years before they actually occurred. As Friedman said himself, there was not "any doubt" that the essay's influence was helped by the fact that it predicted many of the economic problems that would plague Western economies during the 1970s.[7] For this reason, "The Role" is considered one of the most influential papers from one of the greatest economists of the twentieth century.

When we read the paper, we directly confront the central issues of monetary policy: What can adjusting the size of the money supply do? How effective is it? And what are the most useful policy goals?

While some of Friedman's answers to these questions are no longer considered correct, it is still valuable to follow his thinking. It is important to learn to think about questions such as the way changes in the money supply can lead to changes in the level of employment and prices. If we do, we can develop a deeper view of current events such as the controversies that raged over America's central bank, the Federal Reserve,* and its approach to the financial crisis of 2008–2010. The disagreements then revolved around the question of how effective monetary policy can be in returning the economy to a healthy state, particularly in times of crisis—the same question that Friedman addressed in his paper.[8]

Beyond the specific economic lessons in the paper, "The Role" is a wonderful example of logical reasoning. Reading it, students across the academic disciplines will gain an excellent lesson in how a widely held, but possibly misguided, position can be taken apart. Friedman's approach here, and one he often takes in his papers, is to follow each idea of his intellectual opponent to its logical end. In this case, he describes how the Phillips Curve may operate in the short term, but then shows how over time it will be reversed. This kind of argument forces the reader to challenge his or her beliefs and ideas—and offers an opportunity to grow.

1. Milton Friedman, "Autobiography," *Nobel Prize in Economics*, accessed May 12, 2013, http://www.nobelprize.org/nobel_prizes/economics/laureates/1976/friedman-autobio.html.

2. Naomi Klein, *The Shock Doctrine: The Rise of Disaster Capitalism* (Toronto: Knopf Canada, 2009).

3. Milton Friedman, "The Role of Monetary Policy," *American Economic Review* 58, no. 1 (March 1, 1968): 8.

4. Friedman, "The Role": 11.

5. Friedman, "The Role": 16.

6. Friedman, "The Role": 17.

7. Quoted in Brian Snowdon and Howard R. Vane, *Modern Macroeconomics: Its Origins, Development and Current State* (Cheltenham: Edward Elgar, 2005), 204.

8. Stephen Williamson, "Kocherlakota: A Puzzle," accessed February 18, 2015, http://newmonetarism.blogspot.com/2013/09/kocherlakota-puzzle.html.

SECTION 1
INFLUENCES

MODULE 1

THE AUTHOR AND THE HISTORICAL CONTEXT

KEY POINTS

- "The Role of Monetary Policy" touches on a question of huge importance for policymakers. What role, if any, should government—specifically a government's monetary policy*—play in managing the economy?

- Growing up during the Great Depression* left a strong mark on Friedman. He attacked the Keynesian* analysis of the depression. For him, bad monetary policy contributed to the crash.

- The work was written after World War II* when economic policy was under debate. Some argued for central economic planning and strong government intervention, following the Keynesian tradition. Others argued for minimal government intervention as advocated by the "classical" economic tradition.*

Why Read This Text?

Milton Friedman's paper "The Role of Monetary Policy" is a key contribution to macroeconomics*—the study of the economy as a whole—and a short, clear statement of the monetarist* position within that field.

Monetarism was developed in the middle of the twentieth century, mainly by Friedman. It was opposed to the assumption, then widely accepted, that a government can improve the economy by adjusting the size of a country's supply of money—an idea promoted by the followers of the great British economist John Maynard Keynes.*

According to monetarism, this may work in the short run. But in the long run any positive effects such as greater employment will disappear and the attempt will cause more harm than good. The government's main task, said the monetarists, should be to adjust money supply* to keep prices stable.

Originally written as a speech to the American Economic Association in 1967, it had a deep and immediate impact on the attitude of economists towards monetary policy. The speech and the paper that followed it are one of several works that shifted mainstream opinion among economists and policymakers away from the Keynesian position and towards the monetarist position that then held sway in the 1970s.

Friedman's goal was to outline his vision for an effective monetary policy that would help achieve economic stability. For him, stability meant "high employment, stable prices and rapid growth."[1] The title he chose for his address was clear. "The Role of Monetary Policy" argued that monetary policy had a vital role to play in economic policymaking, but that its role and mechanisms were widely misunderstood. Specifically, Friedman argued that the Keynesian economists of the 1950s and 1960s misunderstood the relationship between inflation* and unemployment,* believing that governments could decrease unemployment by allowing inflation to happen.This belief came from an analysis of the Phillips Curve,* a formula that showed a "negative statistical link" between the two variables. In other words, it suggested that if you allow inflation to increase, this will reduce unemployment. Friedman showed with precise logic that this relationship applied, but only for so long. In the long run, he argued, it did not work.

Author's Life

Milton Friedman was born in 1912 in New York City to Jewish* immigrants from Eastern Europe.[2] He described his family as "a rather low-income family that had no particular understanding of the broader world."[3] It is likely that the economic uncertainty of his childhood and early adulthood, at the time of the Great Depression, influenced his approach to economics. In particular, during his early years Friedman developed a strong belief in the "basic forces of enterprise, ingenuity, invention, hard work, and thrift that are the true springs of economic growth."[4]

Although this philosophical orientation is more apparent in some of Friedman's other works, it is relevant to an understanding of "The Role," too. Friedman's challenge to the widely-accepted Keynesian approach to monetary policy is in some ways a call to be more humble about what government can accomplish in terms of improving the economy.

Friedman graduated from Rutgers University in New Jersey in 1932. He specialized in mathematics and was offered two scholarships to do graduate studies: one in mathematics at Brown University and one in economics at the University of Chicago. He chose economics, he recalled later, because the depression made economics seem a more important field of study at the time. He got his MA in Economics from the University of Chicago in 1933 and went on to earn his PhD from Columbia University, New York, in 1946. He then moved back to the University of Chicago, where he continued to teach until his retirement in 1977.[5] He remained active in the field of public policy until his death in 2006.

Throughout his career, both in academia and public debates, Friedman showed an interest in challenging accepted wisdom. And he stayed in the public eye. For example, his much-cited book *A Monetary History of the United States*, co-authored with the economist Anna Schwartz,* was a direct attack against the generally held view about the causes of the Great Depression. In particular, Friedman argued against the position that monetary policy had nothing to do with the crash.[6]

Friedman's attack was so influential that, in 2002, it inspired Ben Bernanke,* then a governor of the Federal Reserve* (one of seven members of the board of governors who oversee America's central bank), to declare:"Regarding the Great Depression.You're right, we did it. We're very sorry. But thanks to you, we won't do it again."[7]

Author's Background

The key economic event of the twentieth century, and a crucial event in the development of later economic thinking and policy, was the Great Depression. It left the American economy shrunken from the stock-market* crash of 1929 to the onset of World War II and had long-lasting effects around the globe. The "laboratory of the depression" is where many of Keynes's key ideas were developed, and most macroeconomists of the twentieth century in some way worked on dealing with that great slump. In 1995 Bernanke wrote: "To understand the Great Depression is the holy grail of macroeconomics."[8]

For Friedman, the impact of the depression was both intellectual and personal. His early life was shaped by the economic turmoil of the period, and his studies took place in the context of economic insecurity. As he writes: "It was taken for granted that I would attend college, though, also, that I would have to finance myself. I was awarded a competitive scholarship to Rutgers University ... I was graduated from Rutgers in 1932, financing the rest of my college expenses by the usual mixture of waiting on tables, clerking in a retail store, occasional entrepreneurial ventures, and summer earnings."[9] With economic catastrophe as his backdrop, Friedman began his academic career in 1932 convinced of the importance of personal initiative over other sources of economic support—an attitude that can be readily seen in "The Role."

1. Milton Friedman, "The Role of Monetary Policy," *American Economic Review* 58, no. 1 (March 1, 1968): 1.

2. Lanny Ebenstein, *Milton Friedman: A Biography* (Basingstoke: Palgrave Macmillan, 2007), 5–12.

3. Brian Snowdon and Howard R. Vane, *Modern Macroeconomics: Its Origins, Development and Current State* (Cheltenham: Edward Elgar, 2005), 199.

4. Friedman, "The Role": 17.

5. Snowdon and Vane, *Modern Macroeconomics*, 198–199.

6. Milton Friedman and Anna J. Schwartz, *A Monetary History of the United States, 1867–1960* (Princeton, NJ: Princeton University Press, 1963).

7. Ben Bernanke, "Remarks," accessed February 18, 2015, http://www. federalreserve.gov/boarddocs/ Speeches/2002/20021108/default.htm.

8. Ben Bernanke, "The Macroeconomics of the Great Depression: A Comparative Approach," *Journal of Credit, Money, and Banking* 27, no. 1 (February 1995): 1.

9. Milton Friedman, "Autobiography," *Nobel Prize in Economics*, accessed May 12, 2013, http://www. nobelprize.org/nobel_prizes/economics/laureates/1976/friedman-autobio.html.

MODULE 2
ACADEMIC CONTEXT

KEY POINTS

* The study of economics is generally divided into two parts: microeconomics*—which looks at the actions of individuals and firms—and macroeconomics*—which looks at the whole economy of a country. Friedman's work is part of the latter group.

* Since the Keynesian* revolution of the 1930s and World War II,* governments and central banks around the world had moved uniformly away from classical economics (according to which an economy is self-regulating) towards policies of more active economic management.

* Friedman was part of the classical economic tradition,* which rejected ideas of government intervention in favor of free-market* capitalism.*

The Work in Its Context

Milton Friedman's paper "The Role of Monetary Policy" discusses economics: the study of the production, distribution, and consumption of goods in society.

According to a famous definition of the subject from the British economist Lionel Robbins,* economics is "the science which studies human behavior as a relationship between given ends and scarce means which have alternative uses."[1] Although Robbins's definition captures the importance of scarcity* in economics, it does not quite show the breadth of the subject. Economics is generally divided into two streams: microeconomics and macroeconomics.

Microeconomics is the study of economic life at the level of individuals and companies. It investigates such questions as how individuals make decisions about consumption and how firms set prices. Macroeconomics, the subject of "The Role of Monetary Policy," is the study of the economy as a whole.

Rather than looking at specific firms or people within the economy, macroeconomists study economic life at the national, regional, and global levels. To do so, they use economic indicators* and other variables such as gross national product* (the value of all the goods and services inside a country's borders at a certain time, sometimes called "gross domestic product"), the unemployment* rate, the exchange rate,* the growth rate,* the interest rate,* and the price level.*

It is worth noting that while these indicators are national or regional variables, Robbins's definition highlights the role of the individual in economics.While changes in interest rates, for example, may make individuals change their behavior, macroeconomists are only interested in behavioral changes that can be shown to operate on a larger scale.

> "If the Treasury were to fill old bottles with banknotes, bury them ... and leave it to private enterprise on well-tried principles of laissez-faire* to dig the notes up ... there need be no more unemployment."
>
> ——John Maynard Keynes, *The General Theory*

Overview of the Field

Modern economics can be traced to the work of the Scottish

political economist Adam Smith* and his book *An Inquiry into the Nature and Causes of the Wealth of Nations* (1776).[2] The model of capitalism* it presents is still relevant today.

Wealth of Nations is in many ways a book about free markets. Writing at a time when "mercantilist"* economic policies (prohibiting trade between nations) were dominant, Smith developed a clear theory that showed how free trade* and the division of labor* (both within a country and between nations) could benefit society.

Smith saw markets as natural to human life. He believed the inclination to "truck, barter, and trade one thing for another"—in other words, to freely exchange goods in a marketplace—was universal.[3] Perhaps most importantly, Smith described an economy in which individuals, acting in their immediate self-interest, produced the best outcomes for society. His famous concept of the "invisible hand" captures this idea: when individuals make decisions to maximize their own well-being, the forces of the market, which he calls the invisible hand, will guide those decisions towards the best outcomes.[4] As Smith writes, referring to an anonymous economic actor (that is, anyone participating in the economy at any level), "by pursuing his own interest he frequently promotes that of the society more effectually than when he really intends to promote it."[5]

While Smith is associated with supporting free markets, many of the famous economists to follow him were critical. Karl Marx's* *Das Kapital* (1867), for example, was a radical critique of free-market capitalism based on the idea that markets led to a concentration of wealth in the hands of capitalists.[6] Marx writes: "Within the capitalist system all methods for raising the social productiveness of labor are brought about at the cost of the individual laborer."[7]

While to a degree Smith saw markets as self-correcting, Marx saw them as engines of inequality between those who owned capital and those who worked for wages.

Another key work in economics is John Maynard Keynes's* *General Theory of Employment, Interest and Money* (1936), which offered a new support for government interventions to stimulate the economy. A central part of Keynes's theory is the idea of aggregate demand.* This is the total demand for goods and services in an economy—or, as Keynes puts it, an economic force that "relates various hypothetical quantities of employment to the proceeds which their outputs are expected to yield."[8]

The idea is vague on purpose. Keynesians believe aggregate demand can be "influenced by a host of economic decisions—both public and private—and sometimes behaves erratically,"[9] meaning somewhat randomly.

Keynesians also believe that when demand falls, bringing the threat of recession, government intervention in the form of fiscal stimulus*—that is, increased government spending on roads, education, the military, and so on—can bring the economy back to its productive potential.

Academic Influences

Friedman did not write "The Role" in an intellectual vacuum. In fact, the paper is widely associated with the Chicago school of economics,* whose guiding idea is the price theory.* At its most basic, price theory holds that in a free market the value of a good or service is determined by the relation between supply and demand, and shown by its price. A simple example is the water and diamonds paradox.

Water has an enormous economic benefit—life depends on it. Diamonds, on the other hand, are considered luxurious but are not necessary for life. The paradox is that the more essential good—water—has a much lower economic value. Price theory can explain this paradox through the principle of scarcity. Prices are set by the relationship between the demand for a good and its scarcity: water is valuable but not scarce, so it is priced lower than diamonds are.

In many ways, particularly in its belief that prices were self-regulating, the price theory of the Chicago school referred back to the "classical" tradition of economics that held sway before the critiques of Marx and Keynes.

Friedman's work also builds on the ideas of the economists Knut Wicksell* and Irving Fisher,* who were central to developing the idea of nominal* and real* interest rates. As Friedman writes: "Thanks to Wicksell we are all acquainted with the concept of a 'natural' rate of interest and the possibility of a discrepancy between the 'natural' and the 'market' rate."[10] To this, Fisher added the difference between real and nominal interest rates.[11]

Fisher stressed the importance of expectations about changes in prices, which Friedman later used as a key idea in "The Role": "Experience shows that the rate of interest will seldom adjust itself perfectly to changes in price level, because these changes are only in part foreseen."[12]

1. Lionel Robbins, *An Essay on the Nature and Significance of Economic Science* (London: Macmillan, 1932), 15.

2. Adam Smith, *An Inquiry into the Nature and Causes of the Wealth of Nations: A Selected Edition* (Oxford: Oxford University Press, 1998).

3. Smith, *Wealth of Nations*, 62.

4. Smith, *Wealth of Nations*, 14.

5. Smith, *Wealth of Nations*, 14.

6. Karl Marx, *Capital: A Critique of Political Economy*, ed. Friedrich Engels (New York: Cosimo, 2007).

7. Marx, *Capital*, 708.

8. John Maynard Keynes, *General Theory of Employment, Interest, and Money*, accessed February 18, 2015, http://cas.umkc.edu/economics/people/facultypages/kregel/courses/econ645/winter2011/generaltheory.pdf.

9. Alan Blinder, "Keynesian Economics," Library of Economics and Liberty, accessed February 18, 2015, http://www.econlib.org/library/Enc/KeynesianEconomics.html.

10. Friedman, "The Role": 7.

11. Irving Fisher, *The Purchasing Power of Money* (New York: Cosimo, 2006).

12. Fisher, *Purchasing Power*, 210.

THE PROBLEM

KEY POINTS

* Although Friedman wanted less government involvement in the economy, he favored a specific role for the national authorities: prudent management of the money supply* by the central bank.

* Friedman's paper was a response to five decades of work by the Federal Reserve* (America's central bank). During this time, two alternate approaches—monetary policy* (adjusting the money supply), and fiscal policy* (adjusting government spending)—fell in and out of favor as the best approach to improving economic performance.

* Friedman argued that governments had placed too much faith in the belief that by adjusting the amount of money available to the economy, it was possible to manage macroeconomic* indicators such as economic growth* and unemployment.*

Core Question

The "role" in the title of Milton Friedman's paper "The Role of Monetary Policy" refers to the part that monetary policy should play in broader economic management and policymaking.

"Monetary policy" refers to the government's regulation of the money supply—that is, either holding back the money in circulation, or printing more bills. Specifically, Friedman wanted to both "stress what monetary policy cannot do" and to "try to outline what it can do and how it can best make its contribution" to broader economic management.[1] He wanted to outline a vision for an effective monetary policy that would help achieve specific goals: namely,"high employment, stable prices and rapid growth."[2]

Alongside this goal, however, is Friedman's true intention: to challenge the economic consensus (that is, the most generally shared assumptions) of his time. Friedman saw monetary policy as just one area in which the government had too much control over the economy. He wanted less government involvement in the economy, and proposed a more limited monetary policy that would convince not only economists but policymakers, too. As he writes: "We are in danger of assigning to monetary policy a larger role than it can perform, in danger of asking it to accomplish, and, as a result, in danger of preventing it from making the contribution that it is capable of making."[3]

> "There is wide agreement about the major goals of economic policy: high employment, stable prices, and rapid growth. There is less agreement that these goals are mutually compatible or, among those who regard them as incompatible .... [t]here is least agreement about the role that various instruments of policy can and should play in achieving the several goals."
>
> —— Milton Friedman, "The Role of Monetary Policy"

The Participants

Friedman's paper is a response to the five decades of monetary history that came before it. The Federal Reserve System*— America's central bank, also known as "the Fed"—was established in 1913 to regulate monetary policy in the United States. It was given the goals of "accommodating commerce and business" and looking after "the general credit situation of the economy."[4] Since the Fed was created, economists and policymakers have had changing views on exactly how effective it is.

During the early 1920s the Fed was praised for its "capacity for fine-tuning" the economy and was credited for the period's "relative stability."[5] Even after the financial crisis of 1929 and the Great Depression* that followed, many observers saw the Fed as crucial to recovery. In 1932, for example, the politician Adolph Sabath* said:"I insist it is within the power of the Federal Reserve Board to relieve the financial and commercial distress." He was referring to the sharp decrease in demand caused by the depression.*[6]

Until this point there had been a widespread belief that monetary policy—adjusting the money supply—could have a significant impact on things such as employment and growth. But this belief lost much of its appeal after John Maynard Keynes's* work was published in the 1930s. Keynes generally favored fiscal interventions (that is, government spending) over monetary actions. In 1934, for example, he wrote: "It is not easy to bring about business expansion merely by monetary manipulation. [Direct governmental spending], however, is infinitely more important and offers in my opinion much greater hopes."

In the 1950s, monetary policy regained a reputation as an important policy tool, largely due to the discovery of the Phillips Curve.* Named after the economist William Phillips,* the Phillips

Curve shows a negative link between inflation* and unemployment: allowing more inflation, in other words, lowers unemployment, while clamping down on inflation leads to more unemployment.[7] Writing on this phenomenon, Phillips concluded:"The statistical evidence ... seems in general to support the hypothesis ... that the rate of change of money wage rates [one way of defining inflation] can be explained by the level of unemployment and the rate of change of unemployment."[8]

Though Phillips's discovery seemed to imply a strong relationship between inflation and unemployment, it was not until 1960 that economists in the United States came to view the Phillips Curve as an effective policy instrument.

That year, the economists Paul Samuelson* and Robert Solow* published a paper in which they estimated the Phillips Curve for the United States. Their conclusion was that an increase in prices of 4 to 5 percent per year "would seem to be the necessary cost of high employment and production in the years immediately ahead."[9]

Although Samuelson and Solow were skeptical of the reliability of the Phillips Curve in the long run, their paper was received as supporting the idea that the money supply could be used to achieve unemployment targets.[10] This is because allowing the money supply to grow brings more inflation, while limiting money supply holds down price rises.

The Contemporary Debate

It has been suggested that the Keynesian* position—widely

followed when Friedman wrote "The Role of Monetary Policy"—was ripe for criticism. Referring to problems with the Phillips Curve, the economist Harry Johnson* wrote in 1970 that Keynes's approach had "suffered from the same major defect as the orthodoxy Keynes attacked—the attempt to explain essentially monetary phenomena in terms of a mixture of real theory and *ad-hoc*-ery" (by which he meant "making it up on the fly").[11] In that sense, "The Role" was well positioned. It was published at the right time, to an audience ready to receive its arguments.

Friedman was very well acquainted with both the history of monetary policy in the United States and shifting academic attitudes towards the role of money in the economy. His 1963 book *A Monetary History of the United States* included rich historical stories and paid a lot of attention to disputes about the direction of policy.[12] So his address to the American Economic Association, the inspiration for the paper, was delivered as a clear attack on the accepted ideas of the period.

Readers of the paper will be able to grasp this history without reading the original sources, as Friedman provides a summary. Still, some knowledge of the evolution of the accepted positions would be helpful for understanding Friedman's intentions. Friedman does not specifically call out his targets by name, referring only to "the views that prevail today."[13] Still, in the context of the speech, it is fair to assume that Friedman's audience were aware of his intended targets.

1. Milton Friedman, "The Role of Monetary Policy," *American Economic Review* 58, no. 1 (March 1, 1968): 5.

2. Friedman, "The Role": 1.

3. Friedman, "The Role": 5.

4. "Federal Reserve Act of 1913," accessed February 18, 2015, http://legisworks.org/sal/38/stats/STATUTE-38-Pg251a.pdf.

5. Friedman, "The Role": 1.

6. Quoted in Milton Friedman and Anna J. Schwartz, *A Monetary History of the United States, 1867–1960* (Princeton, NJ: Princeton University Press, 1963), 409.

7. Alban Phillips, "The Relation between Unemployment and the Rate of Change of Money Wage Rates in the United Kingdom, 1861–1957," *Economica* 25, no. 100 (1958): 283–99.

8. Phillips, "Relation": 299.

9. Paul Samuelson and Robert Solow, "Analytical Aspects of Anti-Inflation Policy," *American Economic Review* 50, no. 2 (1960): 192.

10. Paul Krugman, "The Pigou Effect," accessed February 18, 2015, http:// krugman.blogs.nytimes.com/2013/08/10/the-pigou-effect-double-super-special-wonkish/.

11. Harry Johnson, "The Keynesian Revolution and the Monetarist Counter-Revolution," *American Economic Review* 61, no. 2 (1971): 9.

12. Friedman and Schwartz, *A Monetary History*.

13. Friedman, "The Role": 5.

THE AUTHOR'S CONTRIBUTION

KEY POINTS

* Friedman's prescription was simple: governments should drastically reduce their use of monetary policy* if they wanted to actively manage the economy. Instead, they should aim for a steady and predictable monetary policy.
* Friedman's contribution attacked decades of economic orthodoxy, which viewed markets—the labor market and the price of goods, for instance—as flawed and in need of strong and activist government intervention.
* Friedman's views were very similar to those of another economist, Edmund Phelps.* Neither of them agreed with the commonly held view that deliberately allowing higher inflation* brings lower unemployment,* and vice versa.

Author's Aims

In his paper "The Role of Monetary Policy," Milton Friedman argues that the interpretation of the Phillips Curve* associated with the economists Samuelson* and Solow* is wrong for two reasons. First, it fails to account for differences between nominal* and real* values. (Real values are adjusted for inflation. If your salary goes up by 2 percent in nominal terms, but inflation is 5 percent, then your *real* salary has gone down by 3 percent.) Second, it makes long-run predictions without taking into account people's *expectations* about the economy.

Friedman was not original in identifying these ideas; the Austrian American economist Gottfried Haberler,* for example, pointed to the role of expectations in 1960: "As creeping inflation continues, more and more people will expect further rises in prices and will take steps to protect themselves ... labor unions will ask for high wage increases in order to secure real improvement."[1] What was original about Friedman's argument was that it was clear, logical, and complete.

The paper unfolds over three parts.

First, Friedman provides a brief overview of how government and central bank policy has evolved since the beginning of the twentieth century, offering his own analysis of these policy shifts as he goes. This part of Friedman's paper is supported by his previous work on monetary economics, particularly his 1963 book *A Monetary History of the United States*, which he sometimes refers to merely as "recent studies."[2]

He then goes on to address his core aims. Here, he focuses on two areas in which monetary policy is, he believes, ineffective: setting exchange rates* between the currencies of different countries, and bringing down unemployment.

Lastly, he offers his own views for "how monetary policy should be conducted." A key part of Friedman's argument is his well-known belief in free enterprise and individual responsibility; he refers to these at the end of the paper, writing: "Steady monetary growth would provide a monetary climate favorable to the effective operation of those basic forces of enterprise, ingenuity, invention, hard work, and thrift that are the true springs of economic growth. This is the most that we can ask from monetary policy at our present stage of knowledge. But that much—and it is a great deal—

is clearly within our reach."[3]

Approach

Like most of Friedman's academic work, in many ways "The Role" looks back to the "classical" economic tradition,* according to which an economy was something that regulated itself. Friedman saw the activist policymaking by governments—associated with John Maynard Keynes's* followers—as a betrayal of classical principles. He wanted to reintroduce classical ideas to economics by using a price-based approach.

Since World War II,* the Keynesian* school of thought had been the main approach to economic management in the academic and policy worlds, leading to Friedman's famous 1965 statement that "we are all Keynesians now."[4]

Friedman did not mean his statement to be entirely literal. As he explained, it was an embrace of Keynesian *methods* but not Keynesian *theory*: "We all use the Keynesian language and apparatus," he wrote, referring to Keynes's way of analyzing the economy using aggregate values (that is, the "grand totals" that indicate how an economy is performing).

Whatever he thought of Keynes's method of analysis, however, Friedman made it clear he did not accept the "initial Keynesian conclusions."[5] Specifically, Friedman rejected the idea that changes in the money supply—or any other governmental intervention—could change "natural" levels of unemployment in the marketplace. In this way, Friedman was informed by his embrace of price theory.*

According to price theory, it is the prices of goods and labor—rather than factors that government can control, like the size of the money supply—that should drive market behavior and the real economy.

Friedman's counter-position to Keynes is known as monetarism,* and is based on the following principles:

- long-run monetary neutrality (the principle that, in the long term, money supply *cannot* affect real variables such as unemployment)
- short-run monetary non-neutrality (the principle that, in the short term, changing the size of the money supply *can* bring about changes such as lowering unemployment)
- recognizing the difference between real* and nominal* interest rates
- using measures such as the overall money supply as the basis for analysis.[6]

One important part of the monetarist approach is the view that any kind of price controls (minimum wages, for example) will create market distortions. Monetarism also holds that monetary policy should focus on price stability and that it should be consistent over time.[7]

Contribution in Context

Although "The Role" was an original piece of work in many regards, many of Friedman's observations about monetary policy overlapped with observations about labor-market economics made that same year (1967) by the economist Edmund Phelps.[*8]

Both Friedman and Phelps argued there was no long-run trade-off between inflation and unemployment. In other words they did not agree with the idea—generally accepted by economists at the time and "proven" by the Phillips Curve—that deliberately allowing higher inflation brings lower unemployment, and vice versa. Phelps's paper is more model-based than Friedman's, but also builds on recognizing a difference between real and nominal wages and the idea of expectations. As Phelps writes, if the idea behind the Phillips Curve is accepted, "the expected rate of inflation must be added to it."[9] This is because "workers will only pay attention to real wages"; if they expect inflation to continue, they will demand higher wage increases to make up for inflation, in addition to any real increases in purchasing power.[*] So over time, expectations about costs and wages undermine the Phillips Curve's power to make correct predictions.[10]

A key factor common to both Phelps and Friedman is the idea of a natural rate of unemployment that cannot be changed in the long run by government actions such as pushing up inflation.

Friedman agreed that there were "enormous similarities and tremendous overlaps" between his work and Phelps's analysis. The main difference was that Friedman examined the issue from the angle of monetary policy and interest rates, while Phelps examined the issue from labor-market dynamics and wages. But, he agreed, his and Phelps's "theories are the same."[11]

1. Quoted in James Forder, "The Historical Place of the 'Friedman—Phelps' Expectations Critique," Oxford Economics Discussion Paper Series 299 (July 2008), 6.
2. Milton Friedman, "The Role of Monetary Policy," *American Economic Review* 58, no. 1 (March 1, 1968): 3.
3. Friedman, "The Role": 17.
4. Milton Friedman, "The Economy: We Are All Keynesians Now", *Time*, December 31, 1965.
5. Quoted in Roger Garrison, "Hayek and Friedman: Head to Head," accessed February 18, 2015, http://www.auburn.edu/~garriro/hayek%20and%20friedman.pdf.
6. Bennett McCallum, "Monetarism," *Library of Economics and Liberty*, accessed February 18, 2015, http://www.econlib.org/library/Enc/Monetarism.html.
7. McCallum, "Monetarism."
8. Edmund Phelps, "Phillips Curves, Expectations of Inflation and Optimal Employment over Time," *Economica* 34, no. 135 (1967): 254–281.
9. Phelps, "Phillips Curves," 261.
10. Kevin Hoover, "Phillips Curve," accessed February 18, 2015, http://www. econlib.org/library/Enc/PhillipsCurve.html.
11. Quoted in Brian Snowdon and Howard R. Vane, *Modern Macroeconomics: Its Origins, Development and Current State* (Cheltenham: Edward Elgar, 2005), 205.

SECTION 2
IDEAS

MAIN IDEAS

KEY POINTS

- In his paper, Friedman explores how theories of monetary policy* changed over time, the limits to the things that monetary policy can accomplish, and the theory that it should be conducted modestly.

- Friedman argues that governments expect too much from monetary policy. It cannot control inflation* or unemployment* in the long term, he says—and trying to use monetary policy in this way will eventually cause damage to economic growth.

- The paper is based on a speech Friedman wrote for an American Economic Association conference. He was presenting his ideas to fellow specialists, so assumes they understand the issues, and does not explain them for the non-specialist.

Key Themes

At the center of Milton Friedman's argument in "The Role of Monetary Policy" is the question of how a government can use monetary policy to manage the economy. It is a question that fits within the broader debate between Keynesian* and "classical"* economists, who have very different beliefs about the benefits of government intervention in a nation's economy. Friedman's analysis of this theme revolves around several economic indicators* including the money supply,* interest rates,* unemployment, and prices.

At the time he wrote the paper, policymakers mainly accepted the Keynesian view regarding monetary policy, which backed the use of all mechanisms within a government's control in its attempts to manage the economy, stimulate demand, and keep unemployment low. Friedman sought to show that monetary policy was far less effective than Keynesian policymakers believed and might actually have harmful effects on economic stability.

There are several sub-themes underlying this core theme in Friedman's paper.

The first is the historical evolution of monetary policy and opinions on monetary policy from the 1920s to the late 1960s. In particular, Friedman is interested in the changing attitudes towards the idea that monetary policy can achieve specific outcomes in such things as inflation and unemployment.

In the 1920s, monetary policy was considered highly effective. It was widely held that "a new era had arrived in which business cycles* had been rendered obsolete by monetary technology"[1] (in other words, that management of the money supply would smooth out the economy's booms and busts). In the aftermath of the Great Depression,* however, "opinion swung to the other extreme," and monetary policy was seen as almost completely powerless in the face of economic crisis.[2]

In the 1950s and 1960s, the dominant opinion changed again, and monetary policy was seen as a tool for managing economic outcomes. As Friedman, said: "Today, primacy [in monetary policy] is assigned to the promotion of full employment, with the prevention of inflation a continuing but definitely secondary concern."[3]

Friedman also explores the limits of monetary policy in his

paper, and chooses to focus on two areas in which it is, he believes, ineffective: setting interest rates* and reducing unemployment "for more than very limited periods."⁴ Interest rates and unemployment are central to the overall economy. So by showing them to be areas in which monetary policy has little effect, Friedman is making a strong statement.

Finally, Friedman discusses "how monetary policy should be conducted." He outlines his own preferences for what a central bank should do, inside certain limitations, to maintain a healthy economy.⁵

Friedman's core themes and sub-themes emerge in a logical and clear manner and lead to this idea: that the real goal of government policy should be promoting free enterprise, not managing indicators such as unemployment and inflation.

> *"I therefore shall, as my first task, stress what monetary policy cannot do. I shall then try to outline what it can do and how it can best make its contribution, in the present state of our knowledge—or ignorance."*
>
> —— Milton Friedman, "The Role of Monetary Policy"

Exploring the Ideas

Friedman's main idea in "The Role" is that monetary policy is not an effective tool to achieve long-term inflation or unemployment targets, and instead, the goal of monetary policy should be to "avoid mistakes" and "provide a stable background to the economy."⁶ Specifically, Friedman proposes that monetary policymakers should strive towards "adopting publicly the policy of achieving a steady rate of growth in a specified monetary total"—or in other words, gradually increasing the money supply in a constant and predictable way.[7]

Friedman's suggestion that governments should do no more than aim for steady increases in the quantity of money comes from his doubt that monetary policy can achieve more specific goals. He writes that "the first requirement is that the monetary authority should guide itself by magnitudes [outcomes] it can control, not by ones it cannot control."[8]

Further, he is motivated by his understanding of the causes of the Great Depression* (or "Great Contraction," as he calls it) and his belief that monetary authorities must avoid "sharp swings in policy."[9] As he writes: "In the past, monetary authorities have occasionally moved in the wrong direction—as in the episode of the Great Contraction."[10]

Here, he refers to the sudden decreases in the monetary supply in the immediate aftermath of the financial crisis of 1929. He goes on: "More frequently, they have moved in the right direction, albeit often too late, but have erred [made a mistake] by moving too far."[11]

According to Friedman, if monetary authorities maintained a "steady but moderate growth in the quantity of money," it would contribute to overall economic stability and would make a "major contribution to avoidance of either inflation or deflation* of prices."[12]

Language and Expression

As "The Role" was originally presented as a speech to an audience of economists, it is delivered in a direct and playful style, and assumes some knowledge of how monetary policy works. Friedman's tone is designed to appeal to specialists—and in particular to persuade fellow economists that their usual views are wrong. Friedman frequently uses the pronoun "you" to describe his audience, a stylistic choice unusual for academic papers and one that makes this paper seem more like an informal seminar presentation than an academic work.

Readers will be more comfortable with the paper if they acquaint themselves with the jargon and core ideas of macroeconomics* such as unemployment, interest rates, and exchange rates.* Further, readers should come to the paper with some general knowledge of what monetary policy is—Friedman does not provide definitions or context.

Unlike many economics papers, "The Role" does not use mathematics. But it does, however, rely on tight verbal arguments that readers may struggle with if they are unfamiliar with the ideas. Understanding the difference between nominal* and real* values is central to his argument, for example. But when he discusses this difference, he does so without providing the reader with any summary of what those terms mean.[13]

1. Milton Friedman, "The Role of Monetary Policy," *American Economic Review* 58, no. 1 (March 1, 1968): 1.
2. Friedman, "The Role": 1.
3. Friedman, "The Role": 5.

4. Friedman, "The Role": 5.
5. Friedman, "The Role": 14.
6. Friedman, "The Role": 12–13.
7. Friedman, "The Role": 16.
8. Friedman, "The Role": 14.
9. Friedman, "The Role": 15.
10. Friedman, "The Role": 15.
11. Friedman, "The Role": 16.
12. Friedman, "The Role": 17.
13. Friedman, "The Role": 8.

MODULE 6
SECONDARY IDEAS

KEY POINTS

* The secondary ideas in Friedman's article include an explanation of the weakness of the Phillips Curve:* the fact that it ignores the distinction between nominal* and real* wages. He also examines the "natural rate of unemployment"*—a rate that monetary policy* could not affect in the long term.
* The article gives examples to show the mechanism by which a decision to increase the money supply* would initially fuel economic activity, before the old equilibrium soon re-established itself.
* More attention has been paid to Friedman's views on unemployment in the paper than on interest rates.*

Other Ideas

The most important secondary idea in Milton Friedman's "The Role of Monetary Policy" is his critique of the Phillips Curve— a critique which supports his attack on overly ambitious monetary policy in general.

Friedman's argument centers on the difference between real and nominal wages. Nominal wages are simply the price tag for a good or service. So a worker in 1960 earning seven dollars per hour would have a nominal wage of seven dollars per hour. Real wages, on the other hand, are adjusted for changes in the price level over time. Since price levels* tend to rise due to inflation,* a seven-dollar wage in 1960 would be worth more than a seven-dollar wage a worker earned today, even though the nominal wages are identical. In other words, we are adjusting for *purchasing power*,* which is the amount of goods and services a specific nominal value can buy in a given period. Seven dollars could buy a lot more in 1960 than it can today, so the *real* wage of that worker expressed in 2015 terms would be much higher than seven dollars.

Another important idea in the paper is the "natural rate of unemployment"—in other words, the unemployment rate that would hold when the economy is well balanced.[1] Crucially, for Friedman, the natural rate of unemployment is unaffected by monetary factors—it is related almost exclusively to structural features of the economy such as whether raw materials are available at reasonable prices, or whether there are enough people educated and trained to do all the jobs in the economy. Friedman notes that the natural rate is not fixed, and in fact will change as the structure of the economy changes. For example, Friedman argues that "legal minimum wage rates" and "the strength of labor unions" will have a tendency to increase the natural rate of unemployment by making it more expensive for firms to make new hires.[2] By contrast, "improvements in employment exchanges" and "availability of information about job vacancies and labor supply" will tend to lower the natural rate.[3]

> *"I fear that, now ... the pendulum may well have swung too far, that, now ... we are in danger of assigning to monetary policy a larger role than it can perform, in danger of asking it to accomplish tasks that it cannot achieve, and, as a result, in danger of preventing it from making the contribution that it is capable of making."*
>
> —— Milton Friedman, "The Role of Monetary Policy"

Exploring the Ideas

Friedman praises the Phillips Curve as an "important and original contribution" to economic thought, but challenges its basic defect: its "failure to distinguish between *nominal* and *real* wages."[4] Whereas the Phillips Curve suggests policymakers can target unemployment rates by increasing or decreasing inflation through adjustments of the money supply, Friedman shows that the impact only holds in the short run. Over time, *expectations* about inflation will undo the unemployment targets established in the short run.

To show why, Friedman provides an example. First, assume the monetary authority attempts to set unemployment at 3 percent, which is also assumed to be below the natural rate.[5] Further, assume the economy has most recently gone through a period of stable prices (that is, low inflation) and stubborn unemployment of higher than 3 percent. In order to achieve lower unemployment, the monetary authority "increases the rate of monetary growth."[6] The infusion of cash into the economy will increase spending as lower borrowing costs stimulate business to expand operations, and since one person's spending is another person's income, both spending and income will rise in the economy.

As Friedman notes, the initial effects of this increase will be felt in production and employment rather than in prices: "Producers will tend to react to the initial expansion in ... demand by increasing output, employees by working longer hours, and the unemployed by taking jobs that open up as firms hire more workers to meet the increased demand."[7] Thus, in the short run, the policy has had its desired effect: the infusion of money into the economy increased output and lowered the unemployment rate.

According to Friedman, however, these are only the "initial effects."[8] Over time, the prices that goods sell at will increase in response to the new demand created by the monetary expansion. And this will lower real wages which are, of course, nominal wages adjusted for prices.

Wages tend to increase more slowly than prices, so as the price of goods and services rises, workers' purchasing power will fall. And as workers see their real wages fall, they will demand higher nominal wages. Eventually unemployment will move back to the natural rate as employers cut back the number of people they hire at the new, higher wages. In order for the monetary authority to achieve its target of 3 percent unemployment, it would have to increase the money supply further, which would raise inflation.

According to Friedman, the only way the monetary authority can maintain its target rate of unemployment is with "accelerating inflation"—that is, by constantly increasing it.

Friedman makes a very similar argument for interest rates, showing that monetary policy can do little to maintain interest rate targets in the long run.[9]

Overlooked

Friedman's paper was first delivered as an address to the American Economic Association, the country's foremost professional organization for economists, and later published in the *American Economic Review*, one of the most important economics journals. Given all this initial attention, and the continued attention the paper has received in the decades since its publication, there is little in it that has been overlooked. What is more, it is also a very short work at only 17 pages in length, meaning most informed commentators have thoroughly examined all the ideas Friedman expresses in it.

Since the article's publication in 1968, leading figures in modern macroeconomics,* from the Nobel Prize*-winning economist Paul Krugman* to the economist John Cochrane,* have analyzed it and picked it apart.[10] Interest in different areas of the text has grown and fallen over the years, but Friedman's critique of the Phillips Curve and his support for a steady monetary policy have remained front and center in the discussion.

The one area of the paper that has received relatively less attention is Friedman's discussion of interest rates. Like his critical discussion of the Phillips Curve, Friedman did not think that monetary policy could set interest rates "for more than very limited periods."[11] It is likely that this has received less attention because much of the policy discussion, both when the paper came out and in the debate that followed its publication, focused on employment rather than on interest rates.

1. Milton Friedman, "The Role of Monetary Policy," *American Economic Review* 58, no. 1 (March 1, 1968): 7–8.

2. Friedman, "The Role": 9.

3. Friedman, "The Role": 9.

4. Friedman, "The Role": 8.

5. Friedman, "The Role": 9–10.

6. Friedman, "The Role": 9.

7. Friedman, "The Role": 10.

8. Friedman, "The Role": 10.

9. Friedman, "The Role": 5–6.

10. Paul Krugman, "Who Was Milton Friedman?", accessed February 18, 2015, http://www.nybooks.com/articles/archives/2007/feb/15/who-was-milton-friedman/; and John Cochrane, "The Role of Monetary Policy Revisited," accessed February 18, 2015, http://bfi.uchicago.edu/feature-story/role-monetary-policy-revisited.

11. Friedman, "The Role": 5.

MODULE 7
ACHIEVEMENT

KEY POINTS

* Friedman's article had a big impact. Even leading left-wing* critics agreed that Friedman succeeded in pointing out key weaknesses of the Keynesian* approach, especially by showing that the supposed trade-off between inflation* and unemployment* was only temporary.

* Yet when Friedman's approach to economics, known as monetarism,* was followed by right-wing governments in the US and the UK in the 1980s, the results were mixed.

* Although Friedman remains popular with libertarians,* for others his legacy has been harmed by his association with right-wing figures such as Chile's dictator Augusto Pinochet.* But even his critics think he is a great economist.

Assessing the Argument

Milton Friedman was hugely successful in achieving his aims. His paper "The Role of Monetary Policy" had an immediate influence on the economics profession, even on people who criticized him such as the Keynesian economist James Tobin.* As the Nobel Prize-winning economist Paul Krugman* writes: "Friedman's critique of Keynes became so influential largely because he correctly identified Keynesianism's weak points."[1]

The Swedish economist Erik Lundberg* presented Friedman with the 1976 Nobel Prize in Economics* by saying: "Friedman was the first to show that the prevalent assumption of a simple 'trade-off ' between unemployment and the rate of inflation only held temporarily as a transient phenomenon."[2] Friedman's critique also had a political impact. For example, several chairmen of the US Federal Reserve* Bank were forced to defend their activist policies in the face of Friedman's criticisms. In 1969, Friedman even called for Federal Reserve Chairman William McChesney Martin Jr.* to resign.[3]

The British economists Brian Snowdon and Howard R. Vane write: "While *A Monetary History* has undoubtedly been Friedman's most influential book ... 'The Role of Monetary Policy' has certainly been his most influential article." In 1994, Krugman argued that Friedman's article was "one of the decisive achievements of the post-war era," while Robert Skidelsky* wrote in 1996 that it was "easily the most influential paper on macroeconomics ever published in the post-war era."[4] "The Role of Monetary Policy" remains one of the most heavily quoted papers in economics. Monetarism, meanwhile, went on to strongly influence policy choices in the United States and the United Kingdom during the 1980s as both countries sought to tame inflation. In the UK this was referred to as "[Prime Minister Margaret] Thatcher's* Monetarist Experiment."[5]

> "[It is] very likely the most influential article ever published in an economics journal."
>
> ——James Tobin, economist and frequent critic of Friedman

Achievement in Context

"The Role" has had a deep impact on public policy around the globe.

In 2004, before becoming chairman of the US Federal Reserve, and thereby the most powerful monetary policymaker in the world, Ben Bernanke* noted in a famous speech: "For much of the late 1960s and the 1970s ... many economists and policymakers held the view that policy could exploit a permanent trade-off between inflation and unemployment, as described by a simple Phillips Curve* relationship. The idea of a permanent trade-off opened up the beguiling possibility that, in return for accepting just a bit more inflation, policymakers could deliver a permanently low rate of unemployment. This view is now discredited, of course, on both theoretical and empirical grounds."

Bernanke pointed to Friedman's 1968 article as having "provided a major theoretical critique of the idea of a permanent trade-off," although he pointed out that "scholars disagree about when and to what degree US monetary policymakers absorbed the lessons of Friedman's article."[6]

The results of Friedman's ideas being put into action have been mixed. The experiments with monetarism in the United Kingdom and the United States during the 1980s are widely believed by those on the left of the political divide to have caused mass unemployment and the weakening of the welfare state, particularly in the UK. Significantly, Friedman went on to serve as an unofficial advisor to US President Ronald Reagan* during the presidential campaign of 1980. Despite the widespread adoption of his ideas in the fields of economics and public policy, the ideas Friedman discusses in his article have found limited application in broader fields of study.

Limitations

Reactions to Friedman's work are often tied up with how one feels about his libertarian* political views. In particular, those on the left strongly oppose his belief in minimal state interference in the economy. Human rights advocates, meanwhile, have been highly critical of his promotion of free-market* ideas abroad, particularly his consultations with the notorious Pinochet regime in Chile in the mid-1970s, where Friedman suggested reducing government spending to reduce inflation.[7] Indeed, left-wing protestors interrupted his Nobel Prize ceremony in 1976 on humanitarian grounds.

Recently, the Canadian author Naomi Klein* strongly criticized Friedman in her book *The Shock Doctrine*. In reference to Friedman's support for private education, Klein writes: "For more than three decades, Friedman and his powerful followers had been perfecting this very strategy: waiting for a major crisis, then selling off pieces of the state to private players while citizens were still reeling from the shock."[8]

Those on the libertarian end of the political spectrum, meanwhile, tend to view Friedman's work as a recipe for a more efficient and free society—though they often refer to Friedman's other papers, not "The Role." Academic economists, on the other hand, tend to judge his work on its intellectual merits. Krugman, for example, a prominent critic of Friedman, admits that he was a "great economist and a great man."[9] Depending on one's political and professional background, then, it is possible to interpret Friedman's work in various ways.

---

1. Paul Krugman, "Who Was Milton Friedman?" accessed February 18, 2015, http://www.nybooks.com/articles/archives/2007/feb/15/who-was-milton-friedman/.

2. Quoted in James Forder, "The Historical Place of the 'Friedman—Phelps' Expectations Critique," Oxford Economics Discussion Paper Series 299 (July 2008), 2.

3. Edward Nelson, "Milton Friedman and US Monetary History: 1961–2006," Federal Reserve Bank of St. Louis, Working Paper Series (2007), accessed February 18, 2015, http://research.stlouisfed.org/wp/2007/2007-002.pdf.

4. Quoted in Brian Snowdon and Howard R. Vane, *Modern Macroeconomics: Its Origins, Development and Current State* (Cheltenham: Edward Elgar, 2005), 175.

5. Snowdon and Vane, *Modern Macroeconomics*, 175.

6. Ben Bernanke, "The Great Moderation," presented at the Eastern Economic Association, Washington, DC, February 20, 2004, accessed July 25, 2013, http://www.federalreserve.gov/BOARDDOCS/SPEECHES/2004/20040220/default.htm.

7. Naomi Klein, *The Shock Doctrine: The Rise of Disaster Capitalism* (Toronto: Knopf Canada, 2009).

8. Klein, *The Shock Doctrine*, accessed February 18, 2015, http://www. naomiklein.org/shock-doctrine/excerpt.

9. Krugman, "Who Was Milton Friedman?"

MODULE 8
PLACE IN THE AUTHOR'S WORK

KEY POINTS

* Friedman made important contributions to different fields of economics, including consumer choice* and the history of monetary policy,* in most cases attacking then widely accepted Keynesian* ideas.
* Friedman was a public intellectual who fought openly for governments to adopt free-market* policies.
* "The Role of Monetary Policy" represents one of the author's most important contributions to global monetary policymaking. It was part of a broader body of work that won him the Nobel Prize in Economics* in 1976.

Positioning

"The Role of Monetary Policy" was written at the height of Milton Friedman's academic powers in 1967. Earlier, he had written papers on a variety of subjects in economics, including consumer choice, economic methodology, and monetary history. He worked on many areas of economics in his career, but his ideological orientation in favor of free markets and free enterprise always came through.

One of Friedman's famous early works is the 1957 book *A Theory of the Consumption Function*. In it, he introduced the permanent income hypothesis:* the idea that consumption* (that is, spending on goods and services) in any period is related both to a person's *present* income and their expected *future* income.[1]

This hypothesis was a direct challenge to Keynes's argument that "individuals and households adjust their expenditures on consumption to reflect their current income."[2] In other words, Keynes proposed that an individual's monthly spending habits should only depend on their income in a given month—and therefore if they earn more in any month, they will change their spending and saving patterns. Friedman's model, however, took account of "consumption, wealth, and income"[3] to show that a person's current consumption should be explained by their expectations about their wealth and earnings in the long term. This is just one example of Friedman's strong challenges to Keynesianism.

Friedman's book *A Monetary History* (1963), co-authored with the economist Anna Schwartz,* largely paved the way for "The Role of Monetary Policy." The book marked a basic shift in the understanding of the causes of the Great Depression* (or "Great Contraction," as Friedman referred to it) and changed the course of monetary policy by forcing policymakers to see the importance of money in the overall dynamics of the economy.[4]

Referring to the sharp decline in the money stock (the total amount of money in circulation) that occurred as the economy of the United States contracted, Friedman writes: "It is hardly conceivable that money income could have declined by over one-half and prices by over one-third in the course of four years if there had been no decline in the stock of money."[5]

Before the publication of *A Monetary History*, the leading view—again, a position connected to John Maynard Keynes's*

General Theory—was that monetary policy had little impact on the economy during a crisis. But Friedman's book tracks monetary policy over nearly a century in the United States to support the argument that the Federal Reserve's* decision to limit the amount of money in circulation contributed greatly to the Great Depression.

In addition to his technical work in economics, Friedman was highly visible as a public intellectual. He spoke regularly on public policy topics, including education, drug policy, and foreign policy, nearly always proposing a free-market position. He was also known for his work advising foreign governments, often on monetary issues. In a 1975 letter to the Chilean President Augusto Pinochet,* for example, Friedman suggested he reduce "drastically the rate of increase in the quantity of money" in order to avoid rapid inflation and harm to the economy.[6]

> "The Great Depression, like most other periods of severe unemployment, was produced by government mismanagement rather than by any inherent instability of the private economy."
>
> —— Milton Friedman, *Capitalism and Freedom*

Integration

Friedman has rightly earned the reputation as one of the greatest economic thinkers of all time. The *Economist* magazine has described him as "the most influential economist of the second half of the twentieth century ... possibly of all of it."[7] Ben Bernanke,* who went on to serve as chairman of the US Federal Reserve, described him in the following terms: "Among economic scholars, Friedman has no peer. His seminal contributions to economics are legion, including his development of the permanent-income theory of consumer spending, his paradigm-shifting research in monetary economics, and his stimulating and original essays on economic history and methodology."[8]

With such a towering career, it is difficult to judge Friedman's influence on just one dimension, particularly as his work stretched across many areas of economics and politics. Still, a few themes are found throughout his work.

First, as noted above, many of Friedman's works were produced as attacks on what he called "naïve Keynesianism," which was the dominant economic point of view prior to the 1970s.[9] In that sense, Friedman was an ideologue*—he tended to disagree with Keynes and fought for the view that government should have a limited role in the economy. Within this context, Friedman's work on monetary policy should be seen as just one part of a larger mission to shift economic thinking and policy towards free-market principles.

Significance

Friedman body of work is immense and highly influential. His Nobel Prize in Economics, awarded in 1976, was given "for his achievements in the fields of consumption analysis, monetary history and theory and for his demonstration of the complexity of [economic] stabilization policy."[10] His work on monetary economics is significant to his career, in other words, but it is still only a portion of his work.

In some ways, the continuing significance of "The Role" is tied to the evolution of monetarism* in economic thought. Monetarism's popularity grew in the 1960s, and was given a strong push when Friedman's paper was published in 1968. But its popularity declined in the 1970s and 1980s, according to the economist Bennett McCallum,* as the monetarist idea that money demand was constant gave way to the idea that, in fact, the demand for money "shifted significantly and unpredictably from quarter to quarter."[11] Friedman's support for a constant rate of money growth does not seem workable in a world in which the demand for money goes up and down regularly.

The decline of monetarism is rooted in real world events, too. Between 1979 and 1982, the Federal Reserve attempted a "monetarist experiment" to reduce high inflation rates that had continued during the 1970s and attempted to "hit specified monthly targets for the growth rate" of the money supply.[12] The experiment limited the money supply, which had the effect of increasing short-term interest rates and reducing business activity. The result was the "deepest recession since the Great Depression of the 1930s."[13] This experiment is seen today as having been a necessary "attack on inflation," but observers at the time viewed it as a "macroeconomic* disaster."[14]

While Friedman's suggestion of a steady monetary policy is somewhat out of favor today, the seeds of his ideas, particularly the critique of the Phillips Curve,* remain important.

1. Milton Friedman, *A Theory of the Consumption Function* (Princeton, NJ: Princeton University Press: 1957).

2. "Milton Friedman," Library of Economics and Liberty, accessed February 18, 2015, http://www. econlib.org/library/Enc/bios/Friedman.html.

3. Friedman, *Consumption*, 6.

4. Milton Friedman and Anna J. Schwartz, *A Monetary History of the United States, 1867–1960* (Princeton, NJ: Princeton University Press, 1963).

5. Friedman and Schwartz, *A Monetary History*, 301.

6. Milton Friedman, "Letter to General Pinochet on Our Return from Chile and His Reply," accessed February 18, 2015, http://www.naomiklein.org/files/resources/pdfs/friedman-pinochet-letters.pdf last.

7. "Milton Friedman, a Giant among Economists," *The Economist*, November 23, 2006.

8. Bernanke, "On Milton Friedman's Ninetieth Birthday," accessed February 18, 2015, http://www. federalreserve.gov/boarddocs/ Speeches/2002/20021108/default.htm.

9. "Interview with Milton Friedman," Public Broadcasting Service, accessed February 18, 2015, http:// www.pbs.org/wgbh/commandingheightseights/shared/minitext/int_miltonfriedman.html#7.

10. "Milton Friedman—Facts," Nobelprize.org, accessed February 18, 2015, http://www.nobelprize.org/ nobel_prizes/economic-sciences/laureates/1976/friedman-facts.html.

11. Bennett McCallum, "Monetarism," Library of Economics and Liberty, accessed February 18, 2015, http://www.econlib.org/library/Enc/Monetarism.html.

12. McCallum, "Monetarism."

13. McCallum, "Monetarism."

14. McCallum, "Monetarism."

SECTION 3
IMPACT

THE FIRST RESPONSES

KEY POINTS

- Critical responses to Friedman's paper came mainly from Keynesian* economists. Above all, they attacked Friedman's claim that it was pointless for a government to try to lower the unemployment* rate below what Friedman called its "natural" level.

- In the 1970s, the existence of "stagflation"* (a word acknowledging the stagnation and inflation* affecting certain Western economies) seemed to support Friedman's rejection of the claim—supported by the Phillips Curve*—that you could achieve low unemployment if you were prepared to tolerate high inflation.

- Friedman's call for a steady growth rate for the money supply* is seen today as ineffective. But the monetarism* that he championed has had a big impact, especially the idea that careful monetary policy* can be effective in stabilizing the economy.

Criticism

Much of the critical debate around Milton Friedman's ideas focused on his monetarist views in general, and not the specific argument in "The Role of Monetary Policy." Still, some critics in the Keynesian tradition responded directly to the paper.

One of his most prominent Keynesian critics was James Tobin.* In Tobin's address to the American Economic Association in 1971, he challenged Friedman's understanding of the "natural rate" of unemployment, which is at the heart of the analysis in "The Role." Friedman believed that the natural rate resulted from structural features such as the development of the economy, the education of the workforce, and so on. Tobin questioned the validity of the concept. For him, government action should be able to reduce levels of unemployment below any "natural" rate: "Friedman advised the monetary authorities not to seek to improve upon [the natural rate of unemployment]. But in fact we know little about the existence of [any state of balance] that allows for all the imperfections and frictions that explain why the natural rate is bigger than zero."[1]

In contrast to Friedman's view—that there is an amount of unemployment that a government will simply have to live with, since there is a maximum number of people any economy can employ—Tobin argued the natural rate could be reduced with appropriate government policies.[2]

Friedman was also the target of criticisms from monetarists. Karl Brunner* and Allan Meltzer,* for example, writing in reference to Friedman's ideas on monetary policy in general and not just those in "The Role," saw Friedman's theories as not "a particularly useful basis for [experimental] work."[3] Brunner and Meltzer saw Friedman's theory as too vague, and criticized it for not incorporating experimental findings such as the "variability of the lag of monetary policy"[4] (that is, how long it takes for changes in monetary policy to have an effect on the economy).

> *"Now I am a Keynesian."*
>
> —— US President Richard Nixon, 1971

Responses

Friedman remained firm in his challenge of the Phillips Curve* throughout his career. As a public statement in support of the monetarist position, he dedicated much of his 1976 Nobel Prize* acceptance speech to the topic. In that lecture, he pointed out that he was challenging a view held by most economists: "The 'natural-rate' or 'accelerationist' or 'expectations-adjusted' Phillips Curve hypothesis—as it has been variously designated—is by now widely accepted by economists, though by no means universally."[5]

He then offered a summary, over three steps, of how thinking about the Phillips Curve had changed. His brief history began with the observation of New Zealand economist William Phillips* that inflation and unemployment are inversely linked. The second step was the argument, made independently by Friedman and the economist Edmund Phelps,* that the link between inflation and unemployment was not as simple as Phillips had claimed. The third and final step was what Friedman considered to be the emergence of an upside-down Phillips Curve: "In recent years, higher inflation has often been accompanied by higher not lower unemployment, especially for several years in length."[6] This stagflation—the combination of stagnation and high unemployment with price inflation that plagued the United States and Britain in the 1970s—was seen to support Friedman's critique.

As for his monetarist critics, Friedman accepted their criticisms, noting: "I largely agree with Brunner and Meltzer, who do not comment in any detail on my interpretation of Keynes.* The appearance of disagreement simply reflects their gracious assumption that my objective was more ambitious than it was."[7] In a sign of friendship, Friedman also cited Brunner and Meltzer in his

Nobel Prize address, though he did not mention Tobin or any other Keynesian economists directly.

Conflict and Consensus

Friedman's proposal for a constant growth-rate monetary rule— that is, that the rate of monetary growth should correspond to the approximate long-term growth rate of the economy—has fallen out of favor among policymakers. But monetarism has nevertheless made an enormous and lasting contribution to macroeconomics* and current policymaking. The American economist Bennett McCallum* notes that "most research economists today accept, at least tacitly, the proposition that monetary policy is more useful than fiscal policy* for stabilizing the economy."[8] Furthermore, monetary authorities have largely absorbed Friedman's assertions regarding what monetary policy can and cannot do.

As Kevin Hoover,* an economist whose research focus has included the history of twentieth-century macroeconomics, writes: "The 1970s provided striking confirmation of Friedman and Phelps' fundamental point. Contrary to the original Phillips Curve, when the average inflation rate rose from about 2.5 percent in the 1960s to about 7 percent in the 1970s, the unemployment rate not only did not fall, it actually rose from about 4 percent to above 6 percent."[9] This kind of reversal in the Phillips Curve seemed to challenge Tobin's idea that government interventions in the market can drive unemployment closer to zero.

In addition, as Brian Snowdon and Howard Vane describe it, "perhaps the most important and lasting contribution of monetarism has been to persuade many economists to accept the idea that the potential of activist *discretionary* fiscal and monetary policy is much more limited than conceived prior to the monetarist counter-revolution."[10]

In other words, the experience of recent decades has had a sobering effect on policymakers. Those who believed in the power of governmental economic policymaking before Friedman's paper found out that it is less effective than it seemed to be. In that sense, Friedman won the debate with Keynesianism.

---

1. James Tobin, "Inflation and Unemployment," *American Economic Review* 62, no. 1 (1972): 6.

2. Tobin, "Inflation and Unemployment": 15.

3. Karl Brunner and Allan Meltzer, "Friedman's Monetary Theory," *Journal of Political Economy* 80, no. 5 (1972): 837.

4. Brunner and Meltzer, "Friedman's Monetary Theory," 849.

5. Milton Friedman, "Inflation and Unemployment," Nobel Memorial Lecture, December 13, 1976, accessed February 18, 2015, http://www.nobelprize. org/nobel_prizes/economic-sciences/laureates/1976/friedman-lecture.pdf.

6. Friedman, "Inflation and Unemployment."

7. Milton Friedman, "Comments on the Critics," *Journal of Political Economy* 80 (1972): 907.

8. Bennett McCallum, "Monetarism," Library of Economics and Liberty, accessed February 18, 2015, http://www.econlib.org/library/Enc/Monetarism.html.

9. Kevin Hoover, "Phillips Curve," Library of Economics and Liberty, accessed February 18, 2015, http://www.econlib.org/library/Enc/PhillipsCurve.html.

10. Quoted in Brian Snowdon and Howard R. Vane, *Modern Macroeconomics: Its Origins, Development and Current State* (Cheltenham: Edward Elgar, 2005), 197.

MODULE 10
THE EVOLVING DEBATE

KEY POINTS

- Friedman's work paved the way for important developments in macroeconomics,* including the "rational expectations"* approach, which assumes that people and firms make rational and accurate predictions about things such as inflation.*

- The monetarist* school of economics grew out of Friedman's work. Although it has continued evolving, it is often associated with Friedman's proposal for a steady growth of the money supply*—a proposal that has fallen almost completely out of favor.

- In recent decades, there has been a blending of the monetarist and Keynesian* approaches. Followers are usually referred to as "New Keynesians."*

Uses and Problems

Milton Friedman's "The Role of Monetary Policy" and his other work inspired developments in macroeconomics for several decades. One of the key approaches that emerged out of the paper was the "rational expectations" economics associated with economists such as Robert Lucas* and Thomas Sargent.*

Lucas's paper "Expectations and the Neutrality of Money" (1972) took Friedman's analysis of the Phillips Curve* as its starting point and developed a model in which "all prices are market clearing, all agents behave optimally in light of their objectives and expectations, and expectations are formed optimally"—in other words, people and firms are able to behave perfectly rationally in the economy.[1]

These assumptions are directly related to Friedman's critique of the Phillips Curve in the following way. Friedman showed that the only reason a rise in inflation causes even a short-term increase in employment is that workers do not immediately notice that prices are going up and their wages are losing purchasing power.* In other words, *real* wages are falling, giving employers an incentive to hire more workers. But soon workers pay attention to the inflation and expect that prices will continue to rise. Based on their rational expectations, they in turn demand greater wage increases to bring their *real* wages back up to their former level. At this point, inflation stops bringing higher employment rates.* As Thomas Sargent writes, "rational expectations undermines the idea that policymakers can manipulate the economy by systematically making the public have false expectations."[2]

> "The influence of monetarism on how we all think about macroeconomics today has been deep, pervasive, and subtle."
> —— Bradford J. Delong, "The Triumph of Monetarism?"

Schools of Thought

The monetarist school with which "The Role" is associated has evolved and developed since the mid-1960s. In many ways, the school has been connected to what was seen as the failure of Friedman's proposal for a steadily increasing money supply. As the economist Willem Buiter* noted in 2003:"Friedman's prescription of a constant growth rate for some monetary aggregate* [a stock of money] is completely out of favor today ... and has been for at least a couple of decades."[3] Although most monetary authorities now subscribe to Friedman's central idea of providing a stable monetary background, virtually none supports a fixed rate of money growth.

In other words, Friedman's views about the *role* of monetary policy have been accepted by policymakers and the economics discipline, but his views about the way it should be formulated and carried out have not. As the monetary economist Bennett McCallum notes:"Friedman's constant money growth rule, rather than other equally fundamental aspects of monetarism, attracted the most attention, thereby detracting from the understanding and appreciation of monetarism."[4]

McCallum goes on to argue that the key features of monetarism today came out of Friedman's critique of the Phillips Curve. The primary parts of the monetarist critique to Keynesianism that continue to be viewed as valid today are the distinction between real* and nominal* variables, and the rejection of a "long-run trade-off between inflation and unemployment."*[5]

In Current Scholarship

There is some irony in the fact that in today's economic debates most experts in the monetarist tradition would likely identify themselves as "New Keynesians" due to the blending of monetarist and Keynesian ideas that occurred in the 1980s and 1990s. According to Gregory Mankiw,* one of the most prominent specialists in the New Keynesian tradition, the term refers to economists who responded to the new classical* school of monetarism with "adjustments to the original Keynesian [principles]."[6]

According to Bradford Delong,* an economist most associated with the left of the political spectrum, there are five parts to the New Keynesian approach. Some of these parts come directly from Friedman's monetarism.

First, New Keynesians believe that frictions in the economy—burdensome regulations, for example, or a lack of information on the part of buyers and sellers, among other potential barriers—are the primary cause of economic fluctuations (booms and busts) known as business cycles.*

Second, they believe that "monetary policy is a more potent and useful tool for stabilization than is fiscal policy."

Third, that business cycles are best analyzed as departures from "the sustainable long-run trend."

Fourth, the best way to practice macroeconomic policy is to apply a "rule" rather than to analyze each episode "in isolation."

Fifth, that any approach to stabilization must "recognize the limits of stabilization policy."[7]

The similarities to Friedman's work are clear; his challenge of the Phillips Curve was a reminder of the limitations of policies meant to stabilize the economy. Moreover, Friedman always argued for the relative importance of monetary over fiscal policy. Further, following a general policy rule can be seen as similar to Friedman's proposal of a steady increase in the money supply. As Delong notes:"All five planks of the New Keynesian research program listed above had much of their development inside the twentieth century monetarist tradition, and all are associated with the name of Milton Friedman."[8]

1. Robert Lucas, "Expectations and the Neutrality of Money," *Journal of Economic Theory* 4 (1972): 103.
2. Thomas Sargent, "Rational Expectations," last accessed February 18, 2015, http://www.econlib.org/library/Enc/RationalExpectations.html.
3. Quoted in Brian Snowdon and Howard R. Vane, *Modern Macroeconomics: Its Origins, Development and Current State* (Cheltenham: Edward Elgar, 2005), 196.
4. Bennett McCallum, "Monetarism," Library of Economics and Liberty, accessed February 18, 2015, http://www.econlib.org/library/Enc/Monetarism.html.
5. McCallum, "Monetarism."
6. Gregory Mankiw, "New Keynesian Economics," Library of Economics and Liberty, accessed February 18, 2015, http://www.econlib.org/library/Enc/NewKeynesianEconomics.html.
7. Bradford Delong, "The Triumph of Monetarism?" *Journal of Economic Perspectives* 14, no. 1 (2000): 83–84.
8. Delong, "Triumph": 84.

MODULE 11
IMPACT AND INFLUENCE TODAY

KEY POINTS

* Friedman's paper is still very relevant. Many of its proposals of what monetary authorities should and should not do have been widely accepted.

* Friedman played a broad public role as a top economist, a pioneer of monetarism,* and a cheerleader for free-market* capitalism.*

* The debate remains largely polarized between those who argue for increased government intervention in the economy and those, like Friedman, arguing for less.

Position

Milton Friedman's paper "The Role of Monetary Policy" is still very much a part of the current intellectual debate. Many of its lessons about the "proper" role for a successful monetary authority have been accepted, broadly speaking. But the question of how to conduct monetary policy* itself remains the subject of a highly important and evolving academic and policy debate. It is a question that concerns the entire discipline of economics.

As Friedman highlights in his paper, imagining the economy as a series of interconnected machines, "when [monetary policy] gets out of order, it throws a monkey wrench into the operation of all the other machines."[1] As a result, almost all economists need to account for the role of money and monetary policy at some stage when they address questions such as government spending and international trade.

The economist John Cochrane* highlights the importance of Friedman's ideas in contemporary debates in his essay "The Role of Monetary Policy Revisited." For example, he asks: "How many fallacies like the 1968 Phillips Curve* underlie our current policy experiments?"[2] More specifically, Cochrane notes that current monetary efforts to stimulate the economy such as "quantitative easing"*—the policy of a central bank buying financial assets from commercial banks—may be overly optimistic. In the case of the United States, recently, the US Federal Reserve's* policy of quantitative easing "exploded reserves from $50 billion to $3 trillion. Despite that, [gross domestic product*] has yet to really recover from the recession. You have to question, is this doing any good at all? It's time to think like Friedman and evaluate all these policies, while demanding a basis in clear and simple theories."[3]

> "[It was] one of the decisive achievements of the post-war economics."
>
> —— Paul Krugman on Friedman's prediction of "stagflation"—the combination of rising unemployment* and rising inflation that affected the economies of the United States and Britain in the 1970s.

Interaction

Many of Friedman's ideas have been fully merged into modern economics, and many of those that have not are currently out of favor. For example, there is little intellectual desire to revisit Friedman's constant money-supply* hypothesis.

With that in mind, much of the critical debate around Friedman's impact deals with his political positions and the use of his policies internationally. Many of Friedman's critics are on the left politically, and challenge his promotion of free markets, both in the United States and elsewhere. In part this is due to Friedman's complex identity. Paul Krugman* writes that Friedman took on three roles in his life: the role of "economist's economist," the role of a policy pioneer for monetarism, and the role of "Friedman the ideologue, the great popularizer of free-market doctrine."[4] While the last of these is responsible for most of the criticism he has received, Friedman has been certainly been criticized for his advocacy of monetarism too.

Krugman has also examined the uneven relationship between Friedman and the political right in America:"Friedman, it turns out, was too nuanced and realist a figure for the modern right, which doesn't do nuance and rejects reality."[5] While embracing Friedman in this limited way, Krugman maintains his distance: "I'd argue that the experience of the past 15 years, first in Japan and now across the Western world, shows that Keynes* was right and Friedman was wrong about the ability of unaided monetary policy to fight depressions.* The truth is that we need a more activist government than Friedman was willing to [accept]."[6]

This comment captures Friedman's current place in political and economic debate. To some he is seen as a right-wing villain; to others, a libertarian* hero. But the practical nature of a number of his ideas offers the opportunity for a more nuanced opinion.

The Continuing Debate

Some of Friedman's challengers have suggested that while he may have been well meaning, his proposals have been unsuccessful. In "Milton Friedman: a Study in Failure," an essay published just after Friedman's death, Richard Adams, the Education editor for the British newspaper the *Guardian*, argues that despite his reputation as a great economist, most of Friedman's ideas, including key parts of monetarism, have been political and economic failures.[7] Adams points out that Friedman's proposal that central banks should set fixed rules for growth of the money supply was tried in the 1970s and 1980s, but it was found to be unsuccessful and abandoned."Today, no major central bank directly targets money supply data in setting monetary policy—instead they are far more pragmatic."[8]

Other critics, most notably the writer Naomi Klein,* have challenged Friedman on moral grounds. Referring to Friedman's advisory role in the overhaul of the Chilean economy in the mid-1970s after the right-wing military coup, which she calls "the most extreme capitalism makeover anywhere," Klein suggests that the "rapid-fire transformation of the economy" was an unneeded "shock." Moreover, she says, it was motivated by support for free enterprise rather than a desire to promote social good.[9] Klein's critique is typical of the view of Friedman as the public face of free-market ideology, and the mastermind behind the widespread privatization of public institutions in developing countries in the 1970s and 1980s. Klein describes him as the "grand guru of unfettered capitalism" and credits him with "writing the rulebook for the contemporary, hyper-mobile global economy."

1. Milton Friedman, "The Role of Monetary Policy," *American Economic Review* 58, no. 1 (March 1, 1968): 12.

2. John Cochrane, "The Role of Monetary Policy Revisited," accessed February 18, 2015, http://bfi.uchicago.edu/feature-story/role-monetary-policy-revisited.

3. Cochrane, "The Role."

4. Paul Krugman, "Who Was Milton Friedman?", accessed February 18, 2015, http://www.nybooks.com/articles/archives/2007/feb/15/who-was-milton-friedman/.

5. Paul Krugman, "Milton Friedman, Unperson," accessed February 18, 2015, http://www.nytimes.com/2013/08/12/opinion/krugman-milton-friedman-unperson.html?smid=tw-share&_r=0.

6. Krugman, "Milton Friedman, Unperson."

7. Richard Adams, "Milton Friedman: A Study in Failure," *Guardian*, accessed February 18, 2015, http://www.theguardian.com/commentisfree/2006/nov/16/post650.

8. Adams, "Milton Friedman."

9. Klein, *The Shock Doctrine*, accessed February 18, 2015, http://www.naomiklein.org/shock-doctrine/excerpt.

MODULE 12
WHERE NEXT?

KEY POINTS

* The text remains the starting point for discussions on the role of monetary policy* in broader macroeconomic* stability.

* The tools central banks have at their disposal have expanded, as have the temptations to become involved in broader economic fine-tuning. But there remains the central question of whether short-term gains are outweighed by potential long-term consequences.

* Friedman's text, laying bare the dangers of an overly activist monetary policy, was key to the twentieth century's push back against "excessive" government intervention in the economy.

Potential

The financial crisis of 2008–2010* highlighted the continuing instability of the market economy. It also showed how monetary policymakers are constantly trying to adapt to new information and understandings of how the economy works. It is hard to say how exactly monetary policy will evolve over the coming century, but two points seem reasonably clear. First, Friedman forever changed how monetary authorities view their role in providing a stable foundation for the economy. Second, Friedman's proposal for a fixed rate of monetary growth is unlikely to be tried again, since there is a clear need to use monetary policy to smooth out economic fluctuations (by adjusting the money supply,* as needed).

As the economist John Cochrane* notes, Friedman's paper will likely remain important in the future as a reminder of the limitations of intervention. As management of the economy becomes ever more complex, these lessons will only become more relevant.

Consider, for example, the role of monetary policy in an age when national governments have enormous debt: "Every year [the US] takes in $2.5 trillion and spends $3.5 trillion. We bear an existing debt of $16 trillion, and owe a gazillion dollars in future promises," says Cochrane. "If the Fed decides to tighten monetary policy and set interest rates to 5 percent, on $16 trillion in debt that adds $800 billion a year to the deficit." As the conditions of the economy change and present new challenges for policymakers, "The Role" will serve as a reference point for the lesson that "monetary policy can harm the economy" and that policymakers must tread carefully.[1]

> *"Monetary policy cannot achieve by itself what a broader and more balanced set of economic policies might achieve; in particular, it cannot neutralize the fiscal and financial risks that the country faces. It certainly cannot fine-tune economic outcomes."*
>
> —— Benjamin Bernanke, US Federal Reserve Chairman

Future Directions

One of the economists whose approach to monetary policy somewhat mirrors Friedman's is Raghuram Rajan,* currently serving as the governor of the Reserve Bank of India, that country's central bank. Like Friedman, Rajan's views are motivated by a strong belief in free markets* and skepticism of fiscal policy* (that is, government spending to stimulate the economy). In response to the financial crisis of 2008–2010, for example, Rajan argued for fundamental economic changes such as training more people for the jobs in the new global economy, making the tax structure more favorable to business start-ups, and so on, rather than governmental stimulus programs:

"Today's economic troubles are not simply the result of inadequate demand but the result, equally, of [an environment that is not favorable enough to business and economic growth]. For decades before the financial crisis in 2008, advanced economies were losing their ability to grow by making useful things."[2]

In this contemporary version of a debate between Keynesians* arguing for fiscal stimulus* and free-market supporters arguing for changes to economic fundamentals, Rajan plays the role of Friedman.

Another economist who has shown an approach similar to Friedman's is Naranya Kocherlakota,* currently president of the Minneapolis Federal Reserve—though Friedman and Kocherlakota may not have agreed on principles. In a move that might remind us of Friedman's support for a monetary policy in which gradual price changes are the goal, Kocherlakota has argued that the Federal Reserve* must be more clear about its expectations for meeting its inflation goals. In a recent address, for example, Kocherlakota argued that "price stability" requires a clear explanation of the Fed's timeline for achieving inflation targets.[3]

Summary

"The Role of Monetary Policy" remains a work of extraordinary originality and insight, offering the power to predict future developments. It successfully challenged—and overturned—the theoretical basis of the Keynesian approach that was widely accepted up to then. And it changed the course of monetary policy over the following decades, allowing policymakers to learn from previous mistakes and not worsen economic problems and crises. For these reasons it will continue to be important for both policymakers and students of economics.

It is the strength of Friedman's critical analysis of Keynesian economics that sets his paper apart from other academic work. In a short article of 17 pages, Friedman forcefully challenged the theoretical foundations of decades of policymaking and established the basis for the monetarist school of thought. He changed many widely held assumptions for good.

Readers of the paper will gain insight into the historical evolution of monetary policy in America, as well as an outstanding example of economic analysis. Whereas many economics papers are highly technical and somewhat abstract, "The Role" will prepare people to think about events in the financial press and to better understand the world around them. Further, as Friedman is one of the most important economists of the last century, reading the paper will expose students to some of the most basic questions in the public debate around economics: how important is the government to economic policy, and what kinds of policies can work?

---

1. John Cochrane, "The Role of Monetary Policy Revisited," accessed February 18, 2015, http://bfi. uchicago.edu/feature-story/role-monetary-policy-revisited.

2. Raghuram Rajan, "The True Lessons of the Financial Crisis," *Foreign Affairs*, accessed February 18, 2015, http://www.foreignaffairs.com/articles/134863/raghuram-g-rajan/the-true-lessons-of-the-recession.

3. Naranya Kocherlakota, "Clarifying the Meaning of Price Stability," accessed February 18, 2015, https://www.minneapolisfed.org/ publications/the-region/clarifying-the-meaning-of-price-stability.

 **GLOSSARY OF TERMS**

1. **Aggregate demand:** a term for the total demand for goods and services in the economy at a given time.

2. **Business cycle:** an economic notion describing ups and downs in the economy over a period of several years due to alternating phases of boom (growth) and bust (contraction).These expansions and contractions of the economy tend to seesaw around the economy's long-term growth trend.

3. **Capitalism:** an economic system in which industry and trade are controlled by private citizens with property rights over their goods and services.The forum in which trade takes place is the marketplace.

4. **Chicago school:** a cluster of economists based around the University of Chicago. It is generally characterized by a belief in neoclassical economics, specifically price theory, and a general belief in the power of markets.

5. **Classical tradition in economics:** the first modern school of economic thought, most often associated with Adam Smith, David Ricardo,Thomas Malthus, and John Stuart Mill. The tradition was active from the late eighteenth century to the mid-to late-nineteenth century. Classical economists generally believed markets to be self-regulating.

6. **Consumer choice:** the different products and services that are available to the general buying public.

7. **Consumption:** an economic concept that refers to the aggregate (overall) purchasing behavior in the economy.

8. **Deflation:** the phenomenon of too little money chasing too many goods, resulting in declining prices.

9. **Depression:** a sustained downturn in the economy, typically defined in the United States as a decline in gross domestic product exceeding 10 percent or a recession lasting at least two years.

10. **Division of labor:** the specialization of cooperating individuals who perform specific tasks as part of a production process.

11. **Economic growth:** the increase in output of goods and services that an economy produces over a certain period of time.

12. **Economic indicators:** measurable features of an economy such as inflation or unemployment, expressed as a statistics.

13. **Exchange rate:** the rate at which you can exchange one currency for another.

14. **Federal Reserve:** the central banking system of the United States, which regulates the US monetary and financial system.

15. **Financial crisis of 2008–2010:** an economic crisis that originated in the United States and spread through much of Europe and beyond. It is considered to be the most significant financial crisis since the Great Depression of the 1930s.

16. **Fiscal policy:** the use of governmental spending to influence the economy. Examples include spending on social programs, taxation, and the financing of basic public works projects such as highways and bridges.

17. **Fiscal stimulus:** the policy of increasing governmental expenditure by increasing consumption or lowering taxes, usually with the goal of decreasing unemployment and stimulating economic growth.

18. **Free market:** a system in which goods and services are exchanged in a marketplace mediated by the price system. Free markets are most often distinguished from centrally planned economies.

19. **Free trade:** the policy of not restricting the exchange of goods and services between countries. The opposite of free trade is when tariffs restrict the import and export of goods and services.

20. **Great Depression:** the longest and most severe depression of the twentieth century. It originated in the United States, with the collapse in stock prices in late 1929. Unemployment in the USA reached 25 percent, while other countries saw it rise above 30 percent. In many countries, a prolonged recovery did not occur until the end of World War II.

21. **Gross domestic product and gross national product:** GDP, a leading economic indicator, is the market value of all goods and services within a country's borders at a given time. GNP is the market value of goods and services produced by citizens of a country in a given period, regardless of location. The output of an American-owned factory in Kenya, for example, would be included in the US GNP, but not

the US GDP.

22. **Growth rate:** an increase that is usually measured in periods of time.

23. **Ideologue:** a person who adheres to a particular ideology or doctrine and is firmly entrenched in their position.

24. **Inflation:** the phenomenon of too much money chasing too few goods, resulting in rising prices.

25. **Interest rate:** the cost of borrowing money. The Federal Reserve controls interest rates through the "federal funds rate," or the interest rate for federal funds.

26. **Jewish:** describing a follower of Judaism, a monotheistic religion founded over 3,500 years ago in the Middle East. Today Jews are largely concentrated in Israel and the United States, with smaller populations in dozens of other countries around the world.

27. **Keynesianism:** a school of economic thought that argues that economic markets are not self-correcting. It suggests that activist government policies can help to stabilize the economy through government spending (fiscal policy) and control of the supply of money (monetary policy).

28. **Laissez-faire:** a concept in economics describing the situation in which governments do not intervene in the economy and let markets take their own course.

29. **Left wing:** the part of a political system or party that is traditionally socialist or reforming.

30. **Libertarianism:** a school of political thought that calls for near absolute freedom of individual action with a minimal role for government interference.

31. **Macroeconomics:** the branch of economics that deals with the performance of the economy as a whole.

32. **Mercantilism:** an economic regime practiced in Europe from the sixteenth to the eighteenth century that forbid free trade between countries and encouraged governments to accumulate resources at the expense of their rivals. Adam Smith's *Wealth of Nations*, which argues the benefits of free trade, was a rebuttal of this position.

33. **Microeconomics:** the branch of economics that deals with decision-making

processes at the level of individuals and firms.

34. **Monetarism:** an economic viewpoint that argues that in the short run adjusting the money supply can have a significant impact on economic outcomes such as unemployment, while in the long run it cannot.The monetarism position emphasizes the differences between real and nominal prices, and argues that monetary policy should follow a rulebook to create stable expectations about the economy.

35. **Monetary economics:** the branch of economics that studies the function of money in the economy. A key question of monetary economics is the relationship between various monetary aggregates, such as the money supply, and economic variables, such as employment.

36. **Monetary policy:** the mechanism used to control the supply of money within an economic zone. A policy that increases the money supply is "expansionary," while a policy that decreases it is "contractionary." Monetary authorities pursue policies that maintain stable prices and keep unemployment low. It differs from fiscal policy, which is linked to taxation, government spending, and borrowing.

37. **Money supply:** an economic concept generally defined as the total monetary assets in the economy at a given time.

38. **New Keynesianism:** a school in economics that combines aspects of rational expectations, classical economics, and Keynesian theory.

39. **Nobel Prize in Economics:** also known as the Sveriges Riksbank Prize in Economic Sciences, this is a highly prestigious award given annually to an economist who has made a significant contribution to the subject.

40. **Nominal values:** in economics, nominal values are expressed in historical terms, while real values are adjusted to reflect price and other changes over time. For example, the nominal price of a car in 1930 was much less than the nominal price today, but the real price, in terms of purchasing power, was likely higher.

41. **Permanent income hypothesis:** the idea that consumption (that is, spending on goods and services) in any period is related both to a person's *present* income and their expected *future* income.

42. **Phillips curve:** a measure of the relationship between the rate of inflation and the rate of unemployment. It observed that lower unemployment correlates with a higher rate of inflation, suggesting that there is a trade-off between the two.

43. **Price level:** an index or measure of overall prices in the economy. Changes in the price level are determined by the rate of inflation.

44. **Price theory:** a theory in economics based on the idea that the value of a good or service can be determined by the relationship between its supply and demand.

45. **Purchasing power:** the number of goods and services that can be bought with a given unit of currency.

46. **Quantitative easing:** a monetary policy in which the central bank purchases financial assets from commercial banks, raising the price of those assets and stimulating the monetary base.

47. **Rational expectations:** an economic theory based on the assumption that economic agents make accurate, rational predictions about the future.

48. **Real values:** in economics, real values are adjusted to reflect price and other changes over time while nominal values are expressed in historical terms. For example, the nominal price of a car in 1930 was much less than the nominal price today, but the real price, in terms of purchasing power, was likely higher.

49. **Scarcity:** the economic problem posed by limited resources and unlimited wants. Economists only study scarce resources, as unlimited resources have no inherent economic value.

50. **Stagflation:** an economic term that refers to the situation when high inflation and high unemployment occur simultaneously.

51. **Stock market:** an exchange where financial stocks, shares, and bonds are traded.

52. **Unemployment:** the state that occurs when people who are seeking work cannot find it.

53. **World War II:** a global war from 1939 to 1945 centered in Europe and the Pacific. It was fought between the Allies (United States, Britain, Soviet Union, and others) and the Axis (Germany, Italy, Japan, and others).

PEOPLE MENTIONED IN THE TEXT

1. **Ben Bernanke (b. 1953)** is an American economist and chairman of the US Federal Reserve—the most powerful monetary policy-making role in the world.

2. **Karl Brunner (1916–1989)** was a Swiss economist who was a key member of the monetarist school of economics and a frequent critic of the Federal Reserve System.

3. **Willem Buiter (b. 1949)** is an American-British economist known for his work on monetary economics.

4. **John Cochrane (b. 1957)** is an American economist who is best known for his work linking finance and macroeconomics.*

5. **Bradford Delong (b. 1960)** is an American economist who has made contributions to monetary economics and economic history and is perhaps best known as a prominent blogger.

6. **Irving Fisher (1867–1947)** was an American economist. He has been described as a neoclassical economist—a school of economics based on three core assumptions: People are rational and have discernible preferences based on value; people maximize utility, while firms maximize profits; people act with full and relevant information. He is credited with beginning the school of macroeconomics known as "monetarism."

7. **Gottfried Haberler (1900–1995)** was an Austrian-American economist associated with the Austrian School of Economics, who is perhaps best known for his ideas related to comparative advantage and trade.

8. **Kevin Hoover (b. 1955)** is an American economist who has studied the philosophy and methodology of economics with a particular emphasis on causation.

9. **Harry Johnson (1923–1977)** was a Canadian economist whose work focused on international trade and international finance. He is associated with the monetarist school of economics.

10. **John Maynard Keynes (1883–1946)** was a British economist whose contributions to the theory of macroeconomics were greatly influential to economic policy. He argued against the leading ideas of his day, that economic

slowdowns are caused by a lack of aggregate (total) demand, and that at such times, governments should step in to promote demand by increasing their spending in the economy.

11. **Naomi Klein (b. 1970)** is a Canadian author best known for her books such as *The Shock Doctrine* and *No Logo*, challenging the foundations of global capitalism.

12. **Naranya Kocherlakota (b. 1963)** is an American economist who is currently President of the Federal Reserve Bank of Minneapolis. He is notable for changing his views on monetary policy during the financial crisis of 2008–2010.

13. **Paul Krugman (b. 1953)** is an American economist whose work on international trade earned him a Nobel Prize in 2008. He is also widely known as a commentator on politics and economics for the *New York Times*.

14. **Robert Lucas (b. 1937)** is an American economist known for developing the rational expectations approach to economics and for his association with the Chicago School of Economics.

15. **Erik Lundberg (1907–1987)** was a Swedish economist who served as chairman of the Economics Prize Committee that selects the winner of the Nobel Prize in Economics from 1975 to 1979.

16. **Gregory Mankiw (b. 1958)** is an American macroeconomist known as the author of a popular undergraduate economics textbook, *Principles of Economics*. As a public servant in the United States, Mankiw was the chairman of the Council of Economic Advisors from 2003 to 2005 under President George W. Bush.

17. **Karl Marx (1818–1883)** was a German philosopher whose works *Capital* and *The Communist Manifesto* form the intellectual basis for communism.

18. **Bennett McCallum (b. 1935)** is an American economist whose work applies statistical methods to monetary economics.

19. **William McChesney Martin Jr. (1906–1998)** was an American politician who served as chairman of the Federal Reserve Bank from 1951 to 1970. He served under five different American presidents.

20. **Allan Meltzer (b. 1928)** is an American economist in the monetarist tradition, who from 2012 to 2014 served as president of the Mount Pelerin Society, an organization dedicated to political and economic freedom.

21. **Edmund Phelps (b. 1933)** is an American economist renowned for his work on the sources of economic growth, the savings rate, and price—wage dynamics, leading to his development of the natural rate of unemployment. He was awarded the 2006 Nobel Prize in Economics.

22. **William Phillips (1914–1975)** was an economist from New Zealand whose best-known contribution to economics is the discovery of a negative relationship between inflation and unemployment, known as the Phillips Curve.

23. **Augusto Pinochet (1915–2006)** was the 30th President of Chile who held office from 1974–1990 after overthrowing the elected president in a military coup. He is known for the privatization of the economy during his rule.

24. **Raghuram Rajan (b. 1963)** is an Indian economist and Governor of the Reserve Bank of India. His research areas include banking, corporate finance, and economic development.

25. **Ronald Reagan (1911–2004)** was the 40th President of the United States. As President, Reagan was known for "Reaganomics," a policy of cutting taxes, controlling the money supply, and deregulating the economy in order to increase growth.

26. **Lionel Robbins (1898–1984)** was a British economist who was known for his ongoing debate with John Maynard Keynes and for providing a popular definition of "economics."

27. **Adolph Sabath (1866–1952)** was an American politician who served in the House of Representatives, representing Illinois, from 1907 to his death.

28. **Paul Samuelson (1915–2009)** was an American economist who made significant contributions to macroeconomics and is considered by some the "father of modern economics."

29. **Thomas Sargent (b. 1943)** is an American economist who developed statistical techniques to study the rational expectations hypothesis.

30. **Anna J. Schwartz (1915–2012)** was an American economist. Her most famous work was her collaboration with Milton Friedman on *A Monetary History of the United States, 1867–1960*, which fundamentally changed the understanding of the causes of the Great Depression and monetary economics.

31. **Robert Skidelsky (b. 1939)** is a British economic historian perhaps best known for his three-volume biography of John Maynard Keynes.

32. **Adam Smith (1723–1790)** was a Scottish philosopher and political economist best known for his works *The Theory of Moral Sentiments* (1759) and *An Inquiry into the Nature and Causes of the Wealth of Nations* (1776); the latter is widely considered the first modern work of economics.

33. **Robert Solow (b. 1924)** is an American economist who helped develop the theory of economic growth, specifically the Solow growth model.

34. **George Stigler (1911–1991)** was an economist at the University of Chicago. He is best known for his work on "regulatory capture"—the idea that interest groups use the regulatory powers of government to their advantage.

35. **Margaret Thatcher (1925–2013)** was a British politician and the first woman to have held the office of Prime Minister, a position she occupied from 1979 to 1990. She is associated with policies designed to limit state involvement in the economy and stimulate free enterprise.

36. **James Tobin (1918–2002)** was an American economist who made pioneering studies in finance and the uses of monetary and fiscal policy. He is most associated with the Keynesian school.

37. **Knut Wicksell (1851–1926)** was a Swedish economist. His most influential contribution was his theory of interest, and his work is considered fundamental to macroeconomics.

WORKS CITED

1. Adams, Richard. "Milton Friedman: A Study in Failure." *Guardian*. Accessed February 18, 2015. http://www.theguardian.com/commentisfree/2006/nov/16/post650.

2. Bernanke, Ben. "The Great Moderation." Presented at the Eastern Economic Association, Washington, DC, February 20, 2004. Accessed February 18, 2015. http://www.federalreserve.gov/BOARDDOCS/SPEECHES/2004/20040220/default.htm.

3. ____. "The Macroeconomics of the Great Depression: A Comparative Approach." *Journal of Money, Credit, and Banking* 27, no. 1 (1995): 1–28.

4. ____. "On Milton Friedman's Ninetieth Birthday." Accessed February 18, 2015. http://www.federalreserve.gov/boarddocs/ Speeches/2002/20021108/default.htm.

5. ____. "Remarks." Accessed February 18, 2015. http://www.federalreserve. gov/boarddocs/Speeches/2002/20021108/default.htm.

6. Blinder, Alan. "Keynesian Economics." Library of Economics and Liberty. Accessed February 18, 2015. http://www.econlib.org/library/Enc/KeynesianEconomics.html.

7. Brunner, Karl and Allan Meltzer. "Friedman's Monetary Theory." *Journal of Political Economy* 80, no. 5 (1972): 837–851.

8. Cochrane, John. "The Role of Monetary Policy Revisited." Accessed February 18, 2015. http://bfi.uchicago.edu/feature-story/role-monetary-policy-revisited.

9. Delong, Bradford. "The Triumph of Monetarism?" *Journal of Economic Perspectives* 14, no. 1 (2000): 83–94.

10. Ebenstein, Lanny. *Milton Friedman: A Biography*. Basingstoke: Palgrave Macmillan, 2007.

11. "Federal Reserve Act of 1913." Accessed February 18, 2015. http://legisworks. org/sal/38/stats/STATUTE-38-Pg251a.pdf.

12. Fisher, Irving. *The Purchasing Power of Money*. New York: Cosimo Publishing, 2006.

13. Forder, James. "The Historical Place of the 'Friedman—Phelps' expectations critique." *The European Journal of the History of Economic Thought* 17, no. 3

(2010): 493–511.

14. Friedman, Milton, and Anna J. Schwartz. *A Monetary History of the United States, 1867–1960*. Princeton, NJ: Princeton University Press, 1963.

15. _____. *A Theory of the Consumption Function*. Princeton, NJ: Princeton University Press: 1957.

16. Friedman, Milton. "Comments on the Critics." *Journal of Political Economy* 80 (1972): 906–950.

17. _____."The Economy: We Are All Keynesians Now." *Time*, December 31, 1965.

18. _____. "Inflation and Unemployment." Nobel Memorial Lecture, December 13, 1976. Accessed February 18, 2015. http://www.nobelprize.org/nobel_prizes/ economic-sciences/laureates/1976/friedman-lecture.pdf.

19. _____. "Letter to General Pinochet on Our Return from Chile and His Reply." Accessed February 18, 2015. http://www.naomiklein.org/files/resources/pdfs/ friedman-pinochet-letters.pdf.

20. _____. "The Role of Monetary Policy." *American Economic Review* 58, no. 1 (March 1968): 1–17.

21. Garrison, Roger. "Hayek and Friedman: Head to Head." Accessed February 18, 2015. http://www.auburn.edu/~garriro/hayek%20and%20friedman.pdf.

22. Hoover, Kevin. "Phillips Curve." Library of Economics and Liberty. Accessed February 18, 2015. http://www.econlib.org/library/Enc/PhillipsCurve.html.

23. "Interview with Milton Friedman." Public Broadcasting Service. Accessed February 18, 2015. http://www.pbs.org/wgbh/commandingheights/shared/ minitext/int_miltonfriedman.html#7.

24. Johnson, Harry. "The Keynesian Revolution and the Monetarist Counter-Revolution." *American Economic Review* 61, no. 2 (1971): 1–14.

25. Keynes, John Maynard. *General Theory of Employment, Interest, and Money*. Accessed February 18, 2015. http://cas.umkc.edu/economics/people/ facultypages/kregel/courses/econ645/winter2011/generaltheory.pdf.

26. Klein, Naomi. *The Shock Doctrine: The Rise of Disaster Capitalism*. Toronto:

Knopf Canada, 2009.

27. Kocherlakota, Naranya. "Clarifying the Meaning of Price Stability." Accessed February 18, 2015. https://www.minneapolisfed.org/publications/the-region/ clarifying-the-meaning-of-price-stability.

28. Krugman, Paul. "Milton Friedman, Unperson." *New York Times*. Accessed February 18, 2015. http://www.nytimes.com/2013/08/12/opinion/krugman-milton-friedman-unperson.html?smid=tw-share&_r=0.

29. _____. "The Pigou Effect." Accessed February 18, 2015. http://krugman. blogs. nytimes.com/2013/08/10/the-pigou-effect-double-super-special-wonkish/.

30. _____. "Who Was Milton Friedman?" Accessed February 18, 2015. http://www. nybooks.com/articles/archives/2007/feb/15/who-was-milton-friedman/.

31. Lucas, Robert. "Expectations and the Neutrality of Money." *Journal of Economic Theory* 4 (1972): 103–124.

32. Mankiw, Gregory. "New Keynesian Economics." Library of Economics and Liberty. Accessed February 18, 2015. http://www.econlib.org/library/Enc/ NewKeynesianEconomics.html.

33. Marx, Karl. *Capital: A Critique of Political Economy*. Edited by Friedrich Engels. New York: Cosimo, 2007.

34. McCallum, Bennett. "Monetarism." Library of Economics and Liberty. Accessed February 18, 2015. http://www.econlib.org/library/Enc/Monetarism.html.

35. "Milton Friedman." Library of Economics and Liberty. Accessed February 18, 2015. http://www.econlib.org/library/Enc/bios/Friedman.html.

36. "Milton Friedman—Biographical." Nobelprize.org. Accessed February 18, 2015. http://www.nobelprize.org-/nobel_prizes/economics/laureates/1976/friedman-autobio.html.

37. "Milton Friedman—Facts." Nobelprize.org. Accessed February 18, 2015. http:// www.nobelprize.org/nobel_prizes/economic-sciences/laureates/1976/ friedman-facts.html.

38. "Milton Friedman, a Giant among Economists." *The Economist*, November 23, 2006.

39. Nelson, Edward. "Milton Friedman and US Monetary History: 1961–2006." Federal Reserve Bank of St. Louis, Working Paper Series (2007). Accessed February 18, 2015. http://research.stlouisfed.org/wp/2007/2007-002.pdf.

40. Phelps, Edmund. "Phillips Curves, Expectations of Inflation and Optimal Employment over Time." *Economica* 34, no. 135 (1967): 254–281.

41. Phillips, Alban. "The Relation between Unemployment and the Rate of Change of Money Wage Rates in the United Kingdom, 1861–1957." *Economica* 25, no. 100 (1958): 283–299.

42. Rajan, Raghuram. "The True Lessons of the Financial Crisis." *Foreign Affairs*. Accessed February 18, 2015. http://www.foreignaffairs.com/articles/134863/raghuram-g-rajan/the-true-lessons-of-the-recession.

43. Robbins, Lionel. *An Essay on the Nature and Significance of Economic Science*. London: Macmillan, 1932.

44. Samuelson, Paul and Robert Solow. "Analytical Aspects of Anti-Inflation Policy." *American Economic Review* 50, no. 2 (1960): 177–194.

45. Sargent, Thomas. "Rational Expectations." Library of Economics and Liberty. Accessed February 18, 2015. http://www.econlib.org/library/Enc/RationalExpectations.html.

46. Smith, Adam. *An Inquiry into the Nature and Causes of the Wealth of Nations: A Selected Edition*. Oxford: Oxford University Press, 1998.

47. Snowdon, Brian, and Howard R. Vane. *Modern Macroeconomics: Its Origins, Development and Current State*. Cheltenham: Edward Elgar, 2005.

48. Tobin, James. "Inflation and Unemployment." *American Economic Review* 62, no. 1 (1972): 1–18.

49. Williamson, Stephen. "Kocherlakota: A Puzzle." *New Monetarism*. Accessed February 18, 2015. http://newmonetarism.blogspot.com/2013/09/ kocherlakota-puzzle.html.

原书作者简介

米尔顿·弗里德曼，经济学家，1912 年出生于美国纽约市的一个东欧犹太移民家庭。成年时期遭遇 20 世纪 30 年代的大萧条，对其此后的人生观产生了直接影响。1946 年入职芝加哥大学，讲授经济学理论，并最终成为芝加哥经济学派自由市场思想的首要倡导者之一。曾担任时任美国总统里根和英国首相撒切尔夫人的经济顾问，论著遍及经济学领域诸多问题，并因此荣获诺贝尔经济学奖。2006 年逝世，享年 94 岁。

本书作者简介

尼克·布罗顿曾就读于加州理工学院和伦敦政治经济学院。目前任职于帕蒂兰德研究生院，并担任兰德公司助理政策分析师。他当下的政策研究兴趣包括设计临终关怀的分配方案、消除劳动力市场的技能差距、理解风险投资者的风险偏好等。

约翰·科林斯博士任教于伦敦政治经济学院，现任伦敦政治经济学院智库（LSE IDEAS）国际药品政策项目执行主任。

世界名著中的批判性思维

《世界思想宝库钥匙丛书》致力于深入浅出地阐释全世界著名思想家的观点，不论是谁、在何处都能了解到，从而推进批判性思维发展。

《世界思想宝库钥匙丛书》与世界顶尖大学的一流学者合作，为一系列学科中最有影响的著作推出新的分析文本，介绍其观点和影响。在这一不断扩展的系列中，每种选入的著作都代表了历经时间考验的思想典范。通过为这些著作提供必要背景、揭示原作者的学术渊源以及说明这些著作所产生的影响，本系列图书希望让读者以新视角看待这些划时代的经典之作。读者应学会思考、运用并挑战这些著作中的观点，而不是简单接受它们。

ABOUT THE AUTHOR OF THE ORIGINAL WORK

The son of Jewish immigrants from eastern Europe, economist **Milton Friedman** was born in New York City in 1912. He came of age during the Great Depression of the 1930s, an experience that helped shape his outlook for the rest of his life. In 1946, Friedman joined the faculty at the University of Chicago to teach economic theory, and eventually became a leading promoter of its free-market ideas. He advised President Reagan and Prime Minister Thatcher in the 1980s, wrote about a wide range of economics issues, and won the Nobel Prize in Economics for his body of work. He died in 2006 at the age of 94.

ABOUT THE AUTHORS OF THE ANALYSIS

Nick Broten was educated at the California Institute of Technology and the London School of Economics. He is doing postgraduate work at the Pardee RAND Graduate School and works as an assistant policy analyst at RAND. His current policy interests include designing distribution methods for end-of-life care, closing labour market skill gaps, and understanding biases in risk-taking by venture capitalists.

Dr John Collins is a member of the faculty at the London School of Economics, where he is currently Executive Director of the LSE IDEAS International Drug Policy Project.

ABOUT MACAT
GREAT WORKS FOR CRITICAL THINKING

Macat is focused on making the ideas of the world's great thinkers accessible and comprehensible to everybody, everywhere, in ways that promote the development of enhanced critical thinking skills.

It works with leading academics from the world's top universities to produce new analyses that focus on the ideas and the impact of the most influential works ever written across a wide variety of academic disciplines. Each of the works that sit at the heart of its growing library is an enduring example of great thinking. But by setting them in context — and looking at the influences that shaped their authors, as well as the responses they provoked — Macat encourages readers to look at these classics and game-changers with fresh eyes. Readers learn to think, engage and challenge their ideas, rather than simply accepting them.

批判性思维与《货币政策的作用》

首要批判性思维技巧：评估

次要批判性思维技巧：推理

米尔顿·弗里德曼是历史上最具影响力的经济学家之一，他的思想对于世界各国政府的经济政策有巨大的影响。

弗里德曼作为资本主义及其与民主自由的关系的理论家，是在经济学界和政府制定经济政策时最常被引用的权威学者之一。他的论著现在仍引人关注，因为它们对经济学规律和现状掌握得炉火纯青，而且常常应用高层次的评估和推理技巧来得出精辟论点，使专业人士和非专业人士同样信服。

弗里德曼1968年的论文《货币政策的作用》就是他如何通过批判性思维技巧巩固其影响力和名望的重要例证。这篇论文论及政府的货币政策如何影响经济的问题，涉及就业水平及通货膨胀率，等等。其核心是评价和批判当时被广为接受的货币政策构想——菲利普斯曲线（该构想认为通货膨胀率上升自然会提高就业率），弗里德曼通过系统地指出菲利普斯曲线理论的缺陷和不足，说明为什么事实并非如此，然后他归纳出系统性主张，告知政府的货币政策可以做什么、应当做什么。

虽然当今的经济学家认为弗里德曼的观念有相当大的局限性，但是《货币政策的作用》一文仍是评价和反驳错误论断的法宝。

CRITICAL THINKING AND "THE ROLE OF MONETARY POLICY"

• Primary critical thinking skill: EVALUATION
• Secondary critical thinking skill: REASONING

Milton Friedman was one of the most influential economists of all time—and his ideas had a huge impact on the economic policies of governments across the world.

A key theorist of capitalism and its relationship to democratic freedoms, Friedman remains one of the most cited authorities in both academic economics and government economic policy. His work remains striking not just for its brilliant grasp of economic laws and realities, but also for its consistent application of high-level evaluation and reasoning skills to produce arguments that can convince experts and laypeople alike.

Friedman's 1968 essay 'The Role of Monetary Policy' is a key example of how Friedman's critical thinking skills helped to cement his influence and reputation.The paper addressed the question of how a government's monetary policy affects the economy—from employment levels to inflation and so on.At its heart lies an evaluation and critique of the most widely accepted conception of monetary policy at the time—the 'Phillips Curve'—which argued that increased inflation leads naturally to increased employment. Systematically noting the flaws and weaknesses of the Phillips Curve theory, Friedman showed why this is not, in fact, the case. He then drew up a systematic alternative argument for what governmental monetary policy could and should aim to do.

Though economists now consider Friedman's ideas to have considerable limitations,'The Role of Monetary Policy' remains a masterclass in evaluating and countering faulty arguments.

《世界思想宝库钥匙丛书》简介

《世界思想宝库钥匙丛书》致力于为一系列在各领域产生重大影响的人文社科类经典著作提供独特的学术探讨。每一本读物都不仅仅是原经典著作的内容摘要，而是介绍并深入研究原经典著作的学术渊源、主要观点和历史影响。这一丛书的目的是提供一套学习资料，以促进读者掌握批判性思维，从而更全面、深刻地去理解重要思想。

每一本读物分为 3 个部分：学术渊源、学术思想和学术影响，每个部分下有 4 个小节。这些章节旨在从各个方面研究原经典著作及其反响。

由于独特的体例，每一本读物不但易于阅读，而且另有一项优点：所有读物的编排体例相同，读者在进行某个知识层面的调查或研究时可交叉参阅多本该丛书中的相关读物，从而开启跨领域研究的路径。

为了方便阅读，每本读物最后还列出了术语表和人名表（在书中则以星号＊标记），此外还有参考文献。

《世界思想宝库钥匙丛书》与剑桥大学合作，理清了批判性思维的要点，即如何通过 6 种技能来进行有效思考。其中 3 种技能让我们能够理解问题，另 3 种技能让我们有能力解决问题。这 6 种技能合称为"批判性思维 PACIER 模式"，它们是：

分析：了解如何建立一个观点；

评估：研究一个观点的优点和缺点；

阐释：对意义所产生的问题加以理解；

创造性思维：提出新的见解，发现新的联系；

解决问题：提出切实有效的解决办法；

理性化思维：创建有说服力的观点。

THE MACAT LIBRARY

The Macat Library is a series of unique academic explorations of seminal works in the humanities and social sciences — books and papers that have had a significant and widely recognised impact on their disciplines. It has been created to serve as much more than just a summary of what lies between the covers of a great book. It illuminates and explores the influences on, ideas of, and impact of that book. Our goal is to offer a learning resource that encourages critical thinking and fosters a better, deeper understanding of important ideas.

Each publication is divided into three Sections: Influences, Ideas, and Impact. Each Section has four Modules. These explore every important facet of the work, and the responses to it.

This Section-Module structure makes a Macat Library book easy to use, but it has another important feature. Because each Macat book is written to the same format, it is possible (and encouraged!) to cross-reference multiple Macat books along the same lines of inquiry or research. This allows the reader to open up interesting interdisciplinary pathways.

To further aid your reading, lists of glossary terms and people mentioned are included at the end of this book (these are indicated by an asterisk [*] throughout) — as well as a list of works cited.

Macat has worked with the University of Cambridge to identify the elements of critical thinking and understand the ways in which six different skills combine to enable effective thinking.

Three allow us to fully understand a problem; three more give us the tools to solve it. Together, these six skills make up the PACIER model of critical thinking. They are:

ANALYSIS — understanding how an argument is built
EVALUATION — exploring the strengths and weaknesses of an argument
INTERPRETATION — understanding issues of meaning
CREATIVE THINKING — coming up with new ideas and fresh connections
PROBLEM-SOLVING — producing strong solutions
REASONING — creating strong arguments

"《世界思想宝库钥匙丛书》提供了独一无二的跨学科学习和研究工具。它介绍那些革新了各自学科研究的经典著作，还邀请全世界一流专家和教育机构进行严谨的分析，为每位读者打开世界顶级教育的大门。"

—— 安德烈亚斯·施莱歇尔，
经济合作与发展组织教育与技能司司长

"《世界思想宝库钥匙丛书》直面大学教育的巨大挑战……他们组建了一支精干而活跃的学者队伍，来推出在研究广度上颇具新意的教学材料。"

—— 布罗尔斯教授、勋爵，剑桥大学前校长

"《世界思想宝库钥匙丛书》的愿景令人赞叹。它通过分析和阐释那些曾深刻影响人类思想以及社会、经济发展的经典文本，提供了新的学习方法。它推动批判性思维，这对于任何社会和经济体来说都是至关重要的。这就是未来的学习方法。"

—— 查尔斯·克拉克阁下，英国前教育大臣

"对于那些影响了各自领域的著作，《世界思想宝库钥匙丛书》能让人们立即了解到围绕那些著作展开的评论性言论，这让该系列图书成为在这些领域从事研究的师生们不可或缺的资源。"

—— 威廉·特朗佐教授，加利福尼亚大学圣地亚哥分校

TITLE	中文书名	类别
An Analysis of Arjun Appadurai's *Modernity at Large: Cultural Dimensions of Globalization*	解析阿尔君·阿帕杜莱《消失的现代性：全球化的文化维度》	人类学
An Analysis of Claude Lévi-Strauss's *Structural Anthropology*	解析克劳德·列维-斯特劳斯《结构人类学》	人类学
An Analysis of Marcel Mauss's *The Gift*	解析马塞尔·莫斯《礼物》	人类学
An Analysis of Jared M. Diamond's *Guns, Germs, and Steel: The Fate of Human Societies*	解析贾雷德·M.戴蒙德《枪炮、病菌与钢铁：人类社会的命运》	人类学
An Analysis of Clifford Geertz's *The Interpretation of Cultures*	解析克利福德·格尔茨《文化的解释》	人类学
An Analysis of Philippe Ariès's *Centuries of Childhood: A Social History of Family Life*	解析菲力浦·阿利埃斯《儿童的世纪：旧制度下的儿童和家庭生活》	人类学
An Analysis of W. Chan Kim & Renée Mauborgne's *Blue Ocean Strategy*	解析金伟灿/勒妮·莫博涅《蓝海战略》	商业
An Analysis of John P. Kotter's *Leading Change*	解析约翰·P.科特《领导变革》	商业
An Analysis of Michael E. Porter's *Competitive Strategy: Techniques for Analyzing Industries and Competitors*	解析迈克尔·E.波特《竞争战略：分析产业和竞争对手的技术》	商业
An Analysis of Jean Lave & Etienne Wenger's *Situated Learning: Legitimate Peripheral Participation*	解析琼·莱夫/艾蒂纳·温格《情境学习：合法的边缘性参与》	商业
An Analysis of Douglas McGregor's *The Human Side of Enterprise*	解析道格拉斯·麦格雷戈《企业的人性面》	商业
An Analysis of Milton Friedman's *Capitalism and Freedom*	解析米尔顿·弗里德曼《资本主义与自由》	商业
An Analysis of Ludwig von Mises's *The Theory of Money and Credit*	解析路德维希·冯·米塞斯《货币和信用理论》	经济学
An Analysis of Adam Smith's *The Wealth of Nations*	解析亚当·斯密《国富论》	经济学
An Analysis of Thomas Piketty's *Capital in the Twenty-First Century*	解析托马斯·皮凯蒂《21世纪资本论》	经济学
An Analysis of Nassim Nicholas Taleb's *The Black Swan: The Impact of the Highly Improbable*	解析纳西姆·尼古拉斯·塔勒布《黑天鹅：如何应对不可预知的未来》	经济学
An Analysis of Ha-Joon Chang's *Kicking Away the Ladder*	解析张夏准《富国陷阱：发达国家为何踢开梯子》	经济学
An Analysis of Thomas Robert Malthus's *An Essay on the Principle of Population*	解析托马斯·罗伯特·马尔萨斯《人口论》	经济学

An Analysis of John Maynard Keynes's *The General Theory of Employment, Interest and Money*	解析约翰·梅纳德·凯恩斯《就业、利息和货币通论》	经济学
An Analysis of Milton Friedman's *The Role of Monetary Policy*	解析米尔顿·弗里德曼《货币政策的作用》	经济学
An Analysis of Burton G. Malkiel's *A Random Walk Down Wall Street*	解析伯顿·G. 马尔基尔《漫步华尔街》	经济学
An Analysis of Friedrich A. Hayek's *The Road to Serfdom*	解析弗里德里希·A. 哈耶克《通往奴役之路》	经济学
An Analysis of Charles P. Kindleberger's *Manias, Panics, and Crashes: A History of Financial Crises*	解析查尔斯·P. 金德尔伯格《疯狂、惊恐和崩溃：金融危机史》	经济学
An Analysis of Amartya Sen's *Development as Freedom*	解析阿马蒂亚·森《以自由看待发展》	经济学
An Analysis of Rachel Carson's *Silent Spring*	解析蕾切尔·卡森《寂静的春天》	地理学
An Analysis of Charles Darwin's *On the Origin of Species: by Means of Natural Selection, or The Preservation of Favoured Races in the Struggle for Life*	解析查尔斯·达尔文《物种起源》	地理学
An Analysis of World Commission on Environment and Development's *The Brundtland Report: Our Common Future*	解析世界环境与发展委员会《布伦特兰报告：我们共同的未来》	地理学
An Analysis of James E. Lovelock's *Gaia: A New Look at Life on Earth*	解析詹姆斯·E. 拉伍洛克《盖娅：地球生命的新视野》	地理学
An Analysis of Paul Kennedy's *The Rise and Fall of the Great Powers: Economic Change and Military Conflict from 1500–2000*	解析保罗·肯尼迪《大国的兴衰：1500—2000 年的经济变革与军事冲突》	历史
An Analysis of Janet L. Abu-Lughod's *Before European Hegemony: The World System A. D. 1250–1350*	解析珍妮特·L. 阿布−卢格霍德《欧洲霸权之前：1250—1350 年的世界体系》	历史
An Analysis of Alfred W. Crosby's *The Columbian Exchange: Biological and Cultural Consequences of 1492*	解析艾尔弗雷德·W. 克罗斯比《哥伦布大交换：1492 年以后的生物影响和文化冲击》	历史
An Analysis of Tony Judt's *Postwar: A History of Europe since 1945*	解析托尼·朱特《战后欧洲史》	历史
An Analysis of Richard J. Evans's *In Defence of History*	解析理查德·J. 艾文斯《捍卫历史》	历史
An Analysis of Eric Hobsbawm's *The Age of Revolution: Europe 1789–1848*	解析艾瑞克·霍布斯鲍姆《革命的年代：欧洲 1789—1848 年》	历史

An Analysis of Roland Barthes's *Mythologies*	解析罗兰·巴特《神话学》	文学与批判理论
An Analysis of Simone de Beauvoir's *The Second Sex*	解析西蒙娜·德·波伏娃《第二性》	文学与批判理论
An Analysis of Edward W. Said's *Orientalism*	解析爱德华·W.萨义德《东方主义》	文学与批判理论
An Analysis of Virginia Woolf's *A Room of One's Own*	解析弗吉尼亚·伍尔芙《一间自己的房间》	文学与批判理论
An Analysis of Judith Butler's *Gender Trouble*	解析朱迪斯·巴特勒《性别麻烦》	文学与批判理论
An Analysis of Ferdinand de Saussure's *Course in General Linguistics*	解析费尔迪南·德·索绪尔《普通语言学教程》	文学与批判理论
An Analysis of Susan Sontag's *On Photography*	解析苏珊·桑塔格《论摄影》	文学与批判理论
An Analysis of Walter Benjamin's *The Work of Art in the Age of Mechanical Reproduction*	解析瓦尔特·本雅明《机械复制时代的艺术作品》	文学与批判理论
An Analysis of W. E. B. Du Bois's *The Souls of Black Folk*	解析W.E.B.杜波依斯《黑人的灵魂》	文学与批判理论
An Analysis of Plato's *The Republic*	解析柏拉图《理想国》	哲学
An Analysis of Plato's *Symposium*	解析柏拉图《会饮篇》	哲学
An Analysis of Aristotle's *Metaphysics*	解析亚里士多德《形而上学》	哲学
An Analysis of Aristotle's *Nicomachean Ethics*	解析亚里士多德《尼各马可伦理学》	哲学
An Analysis of Immanuel Kant's *Critique of Pure Reason*	解析伊曼努尔·康德《纯粹理性批判》	哲学
An Analysis of Ludwig Wittgenstein's *Philosophical Investigations*	解析路德维希·维特根斯坦《哲学研究》	哲学
An Analysis of G. W. F. Hegel's *Phenomenology of Spirit*	解析G.W.F.黑格尔《精神现象学》	哲学
An Analysis of Baruch Spinoza's *Ethics*	解析巴鲁赫·斯宾诺莎《伦理学》	哲学
An Analysis of Hannah Arendt's *The Human Condition*	解析汉娜·阿伦特《人的境况》	哲学
An Analysis of G. E. M. Anscombe's *Modern Moral Philosophy*	解析G.E.M.安斯康姆《现代道德哲学》	哲学
An Analysis of David Hume's *An Enquiry Concerning Human Understanding*	解析大卫·休谟《人类理解研究》	哲学

An Analysis of Søren Kierkegaard's *Fear and Trembling*	解析索伦·克尔凯郭尔《恐惧与战栗》	哲学
An Analysis of René Descartes's *Meditations on First Philosophy*	解析勒内·笛卡尔《第一哲学沉思录》	哲学
An Analysis of Friedrich Nietzsche's *On the Genealogy of Morality*	解析弗里德里希·尼采《论道德的谱系》	哲学
An Analysis of Gilbert Ryle's *The Concept of Mind*	解析吉尔伯特·赖尔《心的概念》	哲学
An Analysis of Thomas Kuhn's *The Structure of Scientific Revolutions*	解析托马斯·库恩《科学革命的结构》	哲学
An Analysis of John Stuart Mill's *Utilitarianism*	解析约翰·斯图亚特·穆勒《功利主义》	哲学
An Analysis of Aristotle's *Politics*	解析亚里士多德《政治学》	政治学
An Analysis of Niccolò Machiavelli's *The Prince*	解析尼科洛·马基雅维利《君主论》	政治学
An Analysis of Karl Marx's *Capital*	解析卡尔·马克思《资本论》	政治学
An Analysis of Benedict Anderson's *Imagined Communities*	解析本尼迪克特·安德森《想象的共同体》	政治学
An Analysis of Samuel P. Huntington's *The Clash of Civilizations and the Remaking of World Order*	解析塞缪尔·P.亨廷顿《文明的冲突与世界秩序的重建》	政治学
An Analysis of Alexis de Tocqueville's *Democracy in America*	解析阿列克西·德·托克维尔《论美国的民主》	政治学
An Analysis of John A. Hobson's *Imperialism: A Study*	解析约翰·A.霍布森《帝国主义》	政治学
An Analysis of Thomas Paine's *Common Sense*	解析托马斯·潘恩《常识》	政治学
An Analysis of John Rawls's *A Theory of Justice*	解析约翰·罗尔斯《正义论》	政治学
An Analysis of Francis Fukuyama's *The End of History and the Last Man*	解析弗朗西斯·福山《历史的终结与最后的人》	政治学
An Analysis of John Locke's *Two Treatises of Government*	解析约翰·洛克《政府论》	政治学
An Analysis of Sun Tzu's *The Art of War*	解析孙武《孙子兵法》	政治学
An Analysis of Henry Kissinger's *World Order: Reflections on the Character of Nations and the Course of History*	解析亨利·基辛格《世界秩序》	政治学
An Analysis of Jean-Jacques Rousseau's *The Social Contract*	解析让-雅克·卢梭《社会契约论》	政治学

An Analysis of Odd Arne Westad's *The Global Cold War: Third World Interventions and the Making of Our Times*	解析文安立《全球冷战：美苏对第三世界的干涉与当代世界的形成》	政治学
An Analysis of Sigmund Freud's *The Interpretation of Dreams*	解析西格蒙德·弗洛伊德《梦的解析》	心理学
An Analysis of William James' *The Principles of Psychology*	解析威廉·詹姆斯《心理学原理》	心理学
An Analysis of Philip Zimbardo's *The Lucifer Effect*	解析菲利普·津巴多《路西法效应》	心理学
An Analysis of Leon Festinger's *A Theory of Cognitive Dissonance*	解析利昂·费斯汀格《认知失调论》	心理学
An Analysis of Richard H. Thaler & Cass R. Sunstein's *Nudge: Improving Decisions about Health, Wealth, and Happiness*	解析理查德·H.泰勒/卡斯·R.桑斯坦《助推：如何做出有关健康、财富和幸福的更优决策》	心理学
An Analysis of Gordon Allport's *The Nature of Prejudice*	解析高尔登·奥尔波特《偏见的本质》	心理学
An Analysis of Steven Pinker's *The Better Angels of Our Nature: Why Violence Has Declined*	解析斯蒂芬·平克《人性中的善良天使：暴力为什么会减少》	心理学
An Analysis of Stanley Milgram's *Obedience to Authority*	解析斯坦利·米尔格拉姆《对权威的服从》	心理学
An Analysis of Betty Friedan's *The Feminine Mystique*	解析贝蒂·弗里丹《女性的奥秘》	心理学
An Analysis of David Riesman's *The Lonely Crowd: A Study of the Changing American Character*	解析大卫·理斯曼《孤独的人群：美国人社会性格演变之研究》	社会学
An Analysis of Franz Boas's *Race, Language and Culture*	解析弗朗兹·博厄斯《种族、语言与文化》	社会学
An Analysis of Pierre Bourdieu *Outline of a Theory of Practice*	解析皮埃尔·布尔迪厄《实践理论大纲》	社会学
An Analysis of Max Weber's *The Protestant Ethic and the Spirit of Capitalism*	解析马克斯·韦伯《新教伦理与资本主义精神》	社会学
An Analysis of Jane Jacobs's *The Death and Life of Great American Cities*	解析简·雅各布斯《美国大城市的死与生》	社会学
An Analysis of C. Wright Mills's *The Sociological Imagination*	解析C.赖特·米尔斯《社会学的想象力》	社会学
An Analysis of Robert E. Lucas Jr.'s *Why Doesn't Capital Flow from Rich to Poor Countries?*	解析小罗伯特·E.卢卡斯《为何资本不从富国流向穷国？》	社会学

An Analysis of Émile Durkheim's *On Suicide*	解析埃米尔·迪尔凯姆《自杀论》	社会学
An Analysis of Eric Hoffer's *The True Believer: Thoughts on the Nature of Mass Movements*	解析埃里克·霍弗《狂热分子：群众运动圣经》	社会学
An Analysis of Jared M. Diamond's *Collapse: How Societies Choose to Fail or Survive*	解析贾雷德·M.戴蒙德《大崩溃：社会如何选择兴亡》	社会学
An Analysis of Michel Foucault's *The History of Sexuality Vol. 1: The Will to Knowledge*	解析米歇尔·福柯《性史（第一卷）：求知意志》	社会学
An Analysis of Michel Foucault's *Discipline and Punish*	解析米歇尔·福柯《规训与惩罚》	社会学
An Analysis of Richard Dawkins's *The Selfish Gene*	解析理查德·道金斯《自私的基因》	社会学
An Analysis of Antonio Gramsci's *Prison Notebooks*	解析安东尼奥·葛兰西《狱中札记》	社会学
An Analysis of Augustine's *Confessions*	解析奥古斯丁《忏悔录》	神学
An Analysis of C. S. Lewis's *The Abolition of Man*	解析 C. S. 路易斯《人之废》	神学

图书在版编目（CIP）数据

解析米尔顿·弗里德曼《货币政策的作用》: 汉、英 / 约翰·柯林斯（John Collins）
尼克·布洛顿（Nick Broten）著; 陈虎译. —上海: 上海外语教育出版社,
2020
（世界思想宝库钥匙丛书）
ISBN 978-7-5446-6387-8

I.①解… II.①约… ②尼… ③陈… III.①弗里德曼（Friedman, Milton
1912—2006）-货币政策-货币理论-研究-汉、英 IV.①F820.1

中国版本图书馆 CIP 数据核字（2020）第 055693 号

This Chinese-English bilingual edition of *An Analysis of Milton Friedman's* The Role of
Monetary Policy is published by arrangement with Macat International Limited.
Licensed for sale throughout the world.

本书汉英双语版由 Macat 国际有限公司授权上海外语教育出版社有限公司出版。
供在全世界范围内发行、销售。

图字: 09 - 2018 - 549

出版发行: 上海外语教育出版社
（上海外国语大学内） 邮编: 200083
电　　话: 021-65425300（总机）
电子邮箱: bookinfo@sflep.com.cn
网　　址: http://www.sflep.com
责任编辑: 董　新

印　　刷: 上海叶大印务发展有限公司
开　　本: 890×1240　1/32　印张 6.125　字数 127 千字
版　　次: 2020 年 8 月第 1 版　2020 年 8 月第 1 次印刷
印　　数: 2 100 册

书　　号: ISBN 978-7-5446-6387-8
定　　价: 30.00 元

本版图书如有印装质量问题, 可向本社调换
质量服务热线: 4008-213-263　电子邮箱: editorial@sflep.com